TALKING HARPSICHORDS

TALKING HARPSICHORDS

Rambling Revelations

Alastair McAllister

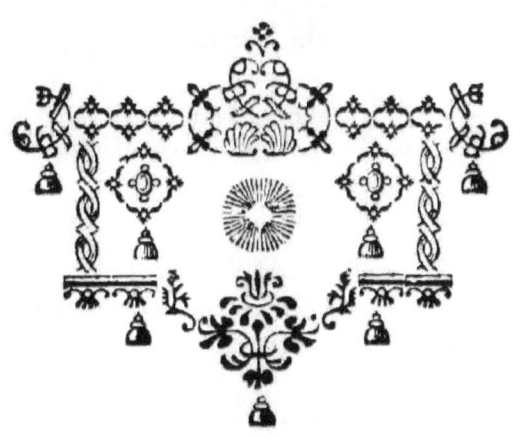

Also by A. R. McAllister

Sonnets and Sundries
Snippets about John Bull

Published by
THE RHYKANE PRESS
20 Albert Street, Preston 3072,
Victoria, Australia.
www.rhykanepress.com

ISBN 978-0-9922872-8-3 (paperback)
ISBN 978-0-9922872-9-0 (hardback)

Set in Bertham Pro, a revival of Frederic W. Goudy's
Bertham typeface produced by typographer
Steve Matteson. Goudy's inspiration was the example
offered him by Lienhart Hol, Ulm, 1482, from the
earliest days of typography. The ornament on the title
page is taken from a book printed in Berlin, 1754,
by Friedrich Wilhelm Marpurg, the German music
theorist, critic, and composer.

Dedication

For my long-suffering but devoted wife Carol and my children

Susan (Sue)
Stuart (Stu)
Catherine (Cath)

for their continuing inspiration.

CONTENTS

PREFACE

I have been encouraged by a number of well-meaning friends to set down some of my thoughts and experiences, along with a requisite number of trials and tribulations, entertained over more than fifty years of instrument building. It is clear that we all now live in a much changed, and effectively smaller, world than presented itself to me in the 1950s. I was unaware, for example, that the late Dene Barnett, in Adelaide, had already cajoled a B. H. P. Co. Ltd. (now BHP Billiton Ltd.) subsidiary into drawing a small quantity of appropriately gauged harpsichord wire for use in the Italian harpsichord he had ordered from Martin Skowroneck, in Germany; for me there was to be no hesitation, no waiting, I wrote to the mother country explaining that I had already begun making a harpsichord, and I needed wire. I still have the reply to my letter of enquiry to Marsh Bros. Sheffield, wherein they asserted that it was not customary for them "to supply music wire in such small quantities, however, as you are a member of the Colonies we will make an exception in this instance." I received the wire, paid their account, and thanked them for their consideration. The rest, as may be said, is history.

Over the years I have received many kindnesses from both customers and colleagues and via reciprocal receptivity have been honoured with their hand of friendship. Such good people all deserve my warmest thanks and best wishes. To single out one individual in particular is hardly fair to the remainder, but in terms of traversing the seemingly endless road to becoming a successful harpsichord maker, the name of Mars McMillan looms large. For more than twenty years we worked closely together creating what some have called the 'Clifton Hill School' of building. (Mars still lives and works in the Melbourne suburb of Clifton Hill and continues, as one might expect, to be one of the most generous people I have ever met!). There are many others I am pleased to recall; sometime makers; Andrew Bernard, Cary Beebe, Richard Ireland, Marc Nobel, Alan Todd, Richard Schaumlöffel, and the late Meredith Moon, and sometime players; Elizabeth Anderson, Paul Dyer, Winsome Evans, Harold Fabrikant, Roger Heagney, Jennifer Paul, Peter Watchorn, and the late Anthony Jennings, and others still, just as special, who have managed, perhaps intentionally, to retain a low public profile. My grateful thanks to one and all!

As the sub-title hints, there may be found in this work, only the requisite amount of rhyme or reason to save one from the ignominy of an Asylum bunk; there is certainly no chronology. It is not an attempt to document a life story, but as much a salute to others, an opportunity to record the issues or events that have interested me, some that have tickled my (some say) quirky sense of humour, and some I consider germane to the art of harpsichord making. Juxtapositions ad nauseam!

To Roger Heagney who read and suggested changes to the work, and made many wise, even salient, observations, go my sincere thanks.

To Andrew Bernard goes abiding appreciation for his effective impersonation of a gadfly, and heartfelt thanks for assisting me with the production of this book, in areas as diverse as mathematics, physics, typography and book design, photography, editing of the text, computer skills, and so on.

I profess myself responsible for any errors, mistakes, misguided or misquoted comments, misrepresentations, etc. for which I would seek understanding.

Last, but not least, it behoves me to thank, sincerely, my family, especially my long suffering wife, Carol, all of whom have given tireless support through times good and not so good.

A. R. McAllister
December 2012

Notation used in this book

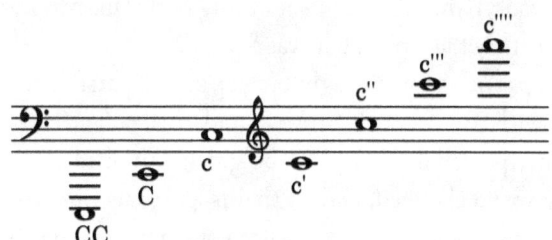

English pitch notation

BILL PAYING TIME

*A chapter oddly brief, for Bill Paying is surely
everyone's lifetime brief*

There can be no doubt that, in some respects at least, I have been cast upon the unsuspecting masses, sadly, if not badly, undercooked. The Scotch College report card I apprehensively proffered my parents (God bless them), recorded, in bold calligraphy; "unaccountable deterioration". (Maybe such a comment cries out to be the subtitle for this book.) There was to be no going back; this was not to be seen as a transitory hiccup! What was I to do?

Perhaps with some thought of deep seated patriotism, my parents banked with The English Scottish and Australian Bank Ltd., so, at that time, perceiving banks to be good, I applied to join. But the banking world changed, and all that is left to us from the wonderful old E. S. & A. Bank is the finance company, Esanda Ltd. In those halcyon days, the 'Scotty' was a pleasure to work for and was noted, especially in Victoria, for the excellence of the architecture of its freehold properties. The Head Office of the E. S. & A., now the ANZ Banking Group Ltd., at 388 Collins St., Melbourne, is an outstanding example, fortunately classified by the National Trust, in its early days, and so preserved for subsequent generations to appreciate and enjoy.

From College directly to Bank 'Training School,' where one of my instructors was to progress, with astonishing rapidity, to eventually become the Bank's General Manager. Can you believe that one of the questions he asked of neurotic young aspirants was; "What is another name for a milking cow?" Miraculously, 'milcher' leapt from mind to paper; I was the only trainee who knew the answer, so it was onwards ever upwards, and at a high speed.

Almost fifteen years were spent with the Bank during which time I married Carol, and the family, Susan, Stuart, and Catherine arrived, in that order, and the bills were all paid. They were good and happy days. As a member of the Bank's 'C' grade table tennis team I managed a premiership flag one year, which quirky whimsy proved to be my greatest (indeed only) sporting achievement. How un-Australian can one be?

Seconded by the Bank to its Industrial Finance Department, which eventually became registered as Esanda Ltd., I started a lunchtime chess club. Its popularity was soon established and a tournament arranged, but I lost in the final, to a chap to whom I had earlier taught the rules. How pathetic! There was a 'five hundred' card playing school too, which thrived for many years; no money changed hands, it was all in the challenge of the play.

I remember my sister, Alison, telephoning excitedly: "Guess what? I've dreamt the winner of the Melbourne Cup!" I knew that she knew nothing about horses, but the word was spread quietly to particular friends, a book was started, a wager laid, and Light Fingers charged home. The next year the phone rang again, another dream: another winner! The third year, yet another dream but this time, she said, not quite so clear cut. An on the nose bet for a win, ran second; the book ran short of funds, and that was that. For a short time I thought I was going to be rich, but it was not to be!

Transferred to the Bank's 'relieving' staff, I will never forget Thornbury Branch, an early casualty to the banks' spates of on again, off again branch closures; (obviously a carefully considered long term policy for, as of 2010, the trend is upwards again, with now an increase in the numbers of new branches being opened, somewhat illogically and often not necessarily in areas of greatest need, as demanded by our ever broadening population explosion). At Thornbury Branch was ensconced one Alan Thornley, the biggest practical joker one would never wish to meet. In those days the banks closed at 3PM and one day, long after 4PM, the Boss called me into his office to enquire what was wrong with my ear. I had no idea, but venturing, as directed, to the washroom mirror, I discovered that Alan (it could have been nobody else) had liberally inked my telephone receiver with stamp pad ink. My ear, and the whole left side of my face looked as if it had been in a brawl with a bottle of Gentian Violet. For several weeks I meditated revenge. Alan was the 'Esanda' clerk and so was provided with a dedicated telephone line, (in those days all phones were black), the rest of the branch members making do with an old PABX system. Whilst Alan was out buying his lunch, I made my move, liberally 'inking' the Esanda phone. That was my mistake! In his office the Boss pushed button A for a line to use his phone, line busy, then button B, line busy, thought, "I'll use Alan's phone." Dear oh dear! Halfway through his conversation the receiver changed sides! Alan returned, lunch carried jauntily under his arm, to espy the Manager with two purple ears and he literally hid in the lunchroom for the rest of the afternoon, packing death, as we used to say. The Boss went home by public transport that night and came to work the next day with baby pink ears. He never mentioned a word about the incident but I was certain it was odds on to shorten a promising career.

The first harpsichord was started whilst still at school, but I continued making, after bank work and at week ends. Being 'posted' to Tooronga branch was very convenient as Mars McMillan had a workshop a couple of blocks away. One day it did actually involve me; an armed robbery! As if out of nowhere there was the bandit brandishing a double barrelled sawn-off shot gun around the banking chamber, and though no-one was shot at, the staff were all petrified (me included). After Police and senior management interviews I rang Mars to tell her I'd been 'held up' at the bank. In a flash came the response: "bullshit." You had to be faster than a speeding bullet to get a line past Mars through to the keeper. But the trip to Police Headquarters to peruse 'mug' files, meant that there was to be no harpsichord making that night.

Sifting through some old school papers recently, I chanced to read the following:

Atop Tank Hill the CUO [Cadet Under Officer] was giving a lecture. "It is claimed," he said, "that with a map, a protractor, and a compass, one can't get lost!" (Cadets look suitably impressed.)

"Well," he added, "I have succeeded in disproving the theory, but that's..." (Cadets wake up completely and the rest is lost in laughter.)

Yes, you guessed it – I was he who gave a map reading lesson in the morning and got the platoon lost in the afternoon. We must have marched for more than twenty miles that day and I recall at one time, the platoon being accosted by a Regular Army Officer in a passing Army vehicle: "Get yourselves that way, (pointing over to the unseen road) right away, you're on a bloody demolition range." "Yes, Sir!"

HOW LUCKY CAN ONE BE?

*So what did trigger the harpsichord obsession; I
assume you may be indulgent enough to ask?*

There I was, listening to the radio in those far off, pre-television, pre-stereo, pre-FM radio, pre-Apple computer, etc. days, when I heard, over the airwaves, some spectacular music played on a wonderful instrument that I had never heard before. My sisters, Alison and Janet, and I were fortunate to be brought up in a musical household, both parents sang and played the piano and Mother had won the very prestigious 'Sun Aria' in 1934, and I have no doubt that, if it had not been for the war when she had to leave London, and later the United States, she would have become a very famous singer indeed. Unfortunately not a single recording of her voice has survived. But to continue; when I asked what I was listening to, my Mother responded without hesitation; it was Domenico Scarlatti, being played on a harpsichord. The ABC (at that time Commission not Corporation) broadcast classical music via Melbourne's classical music station, 3LO (now 774) and when I enquired, they confirmed that the harpsichordist was Englishman, George Malcolm; I immediately determined to obtain my own copy of the record.

H. Rowe and Co., in Elizabeth Street was the only establishment in Melbourne that I knew of that dealt in classical records, the man behind the sales counter, none other than the late, redoubtable John Cargher. No, the album was not available as yet, but he strongly recommended another disc of Scarlatti, played by Wanda Landowska, that she had begun recording after war had erupted in Europe and with the blitzkrieg advancing on Paris. The imported early (and heavy) pressing was labelled 'La Voix de Son Maître,' and yes, it was complete with the famous picture of the dog on the gramophone. In one of the sonatas you can hear the French anti-aircraft guns firing at approaching enemy planes, whilst Landowska, seemingly unfazed, played on. I was hugely impressed! It became my very first harpsichord recording. The recorded sound of the harpsichord was appalling, nothing like that on Malcolm's Scarlatti album, (his was a Decca FFRR, Full Frequency Range Recording, though not yet stereo, the which disc I did eventually acquire), but needless to say I was spellbound by both Malcolm's and Landowska's playing as well as the sounds of their machines.

Recently, I unearthed a saved copy of *The Crippled Gent's Own Book of Humor* an Australian publication printed by Clyde Press, Thornbury, and sold in person on Melbourne's streets in the late 1940s and early 1950s, by incapacitated war survivors, for a small donation. On page eight, the middle page, without any preamble, we read:

> I suppose you would call Mr George Malcolm an infant prodigy. At the age of 29 he became the Master of the Cathedral Music at Westminster Cathedral. The reason we presume to call him an 'infant prodigy' is that as few people know, he began to compose music at the age of about four. At three he could play the violin and at seven he got a scholarship at the Royal College of Music.

The opposite page records:

> "No," said the young lady, scornfully, "when I marry, it must be to a polished, upright, grand man." "It seems to me," replied the rejected swain, "that what you require is a piano."

How very odd! I fancy me I do recall the act of donating a small sum of money for my copy, probably sixpence or a shilling, but the precise amount, I can't remember...

Determined to find out more about these harpsichords I went to the State Museum, then housed in the State Library building in Latrobe St. Melbourne, wherein I discovered a two manual Schudi and Broadwood instrument, dated 1772, complete with its Venetian Swell and Machine Stop. It remains a very important part of the Connell Collection and was originally seen by me just inside two massive doors that opened directly on to Latrobe Street, City. From time to time, the poor unresisting harpsichord was pushed unceremoniously out of the doorway so as to admit artworks and artefacts into the building. No doubt making a complete nuisance of myself, and in my school uniform, I complained to the Director, Dr. Eric (later Sir Eric) Westbrook. He listened! The instrument was moved to a more harpsichord friendly position, where it was roped off, provided with a clear Perspex cover for the keys, and presented to the public a large poster sign which read, 'PLEASE DO NOT TOUCH.' I was content.

One evening whilst at tea, the phone rang for me. It was Dr. Westbrook; one of his important patrons had a harpsichord that needed attention. She asked if he knew of anybody who could help, he said he only knew of me and the call was to see if I would be willing to go to Holbrook, NSW, to assist. Sensing an opportunity too good to refuse, I agreed. As it transpired, it was not a harpsichord at all, but an eighteenth century 'square piano' made by George Astor in London. The disappointment of my hostess was such that I boldly offered to make her a real harpsichord: to my surprise she agreed, and three years later I had finished instrument number one, for the late Mrs. Douglas Carnegie and her daughter Jane. It was thought at the time to be a newsworthy achievement and found its way into the Melbourne press including The Australian Women's Weekly complete with a photograph of myself with Mrs. Carnegie, and Sir Bernard Heinze, who was at that time, conductor of the Melbourne Symphony Orchestra. Mrs Carnegie, as may be imagined, remains permanently enthroned as a hero.

I had not yet met Mars McMillan but she spotted the news items and sought me out; she was three quarters of the way through making an instrument for herself and was at the point of designing a jack to be moulded in plastic. We went on from there; Mars drew up some beautiful (and I mean exactly that), engineers drawings and the first run of jacks was made, in a white acrylic plastic. The new homopolymer, 'Delrin,' was yet to be available in Australia, being patented (by DuPont Industries) in 1960. In practice the acrylic was found to be too brittle, and in due course, the drawings were modified and a second moulding run was organised when Delrin became available. Plastic jacks we thought to be the best thing since sliced beetroot: nowadays almost every maker, myself and Mars included, has reverted to good, old, ever reliable wood.

Wolfgang Zuckermann's book, The Modern Harpsichord, was published in 1969, and Mars and I rated a mention which prompted an expatriate, the late Meredith Moon, then a secretary to the Bodleian Library, Oxford, to write out of the blue that he was considering returning to Australia as he felt that 19 years away was long enough. Meredith was a genuinely funny man and, in an early letter, wrote: "God Almighty! I've been playing some of Bach's inventions: one can tell from Bach's music he was a dirty old man, first with the right hand, then with the left hand, then both hands together." Clearly an 'Aussie' at heart: so home he came! Meredith's arrival prompted the question as to what we might call the expanded work force to which Mars responded: "Why not Mars, Moon, and Uranus?" "Oh no," Richard Ireland, was emphatic, "that would be far too obvious!" Meredith 'played many a Scarlatti sonata on the door knocker,' but moved on to lecturer in Music History at the Melbourne University Conservatorium, where nonplussed notables were accused, to their faces, of being nothing other than "victims of the printed note" or more brusquely, "bloody fools!"

Around this time, Richard Ireland and I started working together and we became good friends. A tad older and much wiser than I, Richard has a great command of the English language and a ready wit, devastatingly ready on occasion! He and his father had built a workshop and we worked closely on a number of instruments, all worthwhile. Richard and Meredith together were something else again. Richard: "Oh no Meredith, that instrument is far too heavily strung, it should be strung with gossamer fine wire!" Meredith: "God Almighty, Richard, it would sound like a cobweb!"

Acting on a premise that was being promulgated by the pundits of the moment, namely: 'that Ruckers harpsichords were pitched about a tone lower than modern pitch,' Richard and I calculated, long hand, the string lengths for an instrument speaking at 440 Hz. Two Italians, after Baffo, and incorporating this scaling, but using iron wire, were considered to have cracked the tonal sound barrier. As Richard observed: "was the scaling the secret to 'real true sound,' or were we simply bewitched by Telefunken's Royal Sound Stereo" to be heard on Leonhardt's recordings? The pathway to enlightenment would continue to prove long and laborious.

I had met Richard at one of the Christ Church South Yarra Bach Festivals. This Festival was established by the Church's organist, the late Leonard Fullard, and was to continue for thirty seven years before Mr. Fullard's eventual demise. I remember one year the phone ringing, Mars answering, and then handing the receiver to me: "It's Leonard Fullard, for you." Taking the phone, I said at once: "Good morning Mr. Fullard," to which he responded in his dry monotone: "Good morning, Mr. McAllister, it's Leonard Fullard speaking." We are still amused: but his dedication to music deserves the highest praise.

It was at the Christ Church 'Bach Festival' that I first heard the late Mancell Kirby play Bach's Goldberg Variations on her Maendler-Schramm. She was Australia's first harpsichordist and had purchased the Maendler, (Schramm was the piano maker in the partnership), when on a trip to Europe with her husband, Dr Reginald Ellery, in the 1930s. As an inquisitive young upstart, I found her forceful personality somewhat daunting but this concealed a kindly disposition and I was privileged to make some home visits when I was shown the Maendler stripped down to its component parts. She owned three instruments and was fluent in three languages; I felt privileged indeed. The notes in her diary of war time performances give no suggestion that she saw anything at all remarkable in presenting programmes of seventeenth and eighteenth century English and French music, on a twentieth century German harpsichord, over Radio Australia, for the ears of Australian troops fighting the Japanese, in tropical Papua New Guinea. Mancell Kirby nearly lived out the century whilst the Maendler now belongs to a collector who lives outside Melbourne, and I understand it is now housed in the gentleman's private museum in China. I feel it is more than a fragment of Australia's musical history, and lost to the highest bidder, as will be revealed.

Mancell's husband, Doctor Reginald Ellery, is remembered as a pioneering psychiatrist. I never met him, but his autobiography, *The Cow Jumped Over the Moon*, is one of the most elegantly crafted works I have read. Mrs Ellery had insisted I read it. Eventually borrowing a copy from the local library, I learned that the Ellerys had earlier resided in the same street, just two doors away from where Carol and I had first set up home. I empathised with the author's description of his walking past our front gate to the tram stop in Cotham Road, Kew, purchasing a copy of the morning broadsheet, (which was obtained from a small 'coin in the slot' dispenser at the tram stop), climbing onto the tram, and unfolding his paper, to reveal the front page news of his dismissal as head of psychiatry at Melbourne's Royal Prince Alfred Hospital. He had been branded by whisperers as a communist, and this was altogether too much for the bureaucracy, who summarily gave him the chop, with not a word to his face nor a question asked! This was surely bureaucratic bastardry at its worst, and dealt out to a man who, before the War, had been the very successful head of Victoria's Lunacy Department, as it was then known. Each chapter in the book quoted a line from a nursery rhyme as its chapter heading, for example, *There was a Crooked Man*, detailed his fight against the crippling pain of arthritis. It is an important and moving summary of a remarkable life and a strongly recommended read.

The Maendler-Schramm harpsichord, I now realise, was the ultimate 'blunderbuss' of its genre, but when I was first introduced to it I was, literally, 'gob smacked.' As Zuckermann records, they were 'extremely complicated' beasts; this one of Mancell's was the most complicated model that Maendler was to make, and was equipped with no less than eight pedals. It was also, as might be expected, provided with overhead dampers; the eighth pedal, (on the far right) controlled these, and made possible a piano like sustain. This sustaining pedal worked on the lower manual 8' and 16' only, and the feat was accomplished by the fact that the plectra in those registers did not touch the strings when the jacks returned to their rest position, (as the player took his finger from the keys). In the other jacks the plectra touched the string on their return, in the usual manner. Though doubtless a fiddle to maintain in perfect regulation, the design of the special jacks remains a brilliant concept, and, as I recall, certainly did 'something' for Bach's Chromatic Fantasy when Mancell played it for me. With the two keyboards uncoupled, you could play a genuine sustained legato on the lower one against a staccato on the upper. I confess it made such an impression on me that my first harpsichord, for the Carnegies, had the full iron frame and four pedals; 2×8', buff stop, and lastly the 'celestial harp' stop, where one of the pedals lifted all the jacks, and therefore their dampers, clear of the strings allowing a sympathetic sustain. I have since made another instrument for Jane, the first, I believe, finding its way inland, to Broken Hill, where, I confess, I can only hope it has suffered the ignominy of being whisked off by a willy-willy!

There remains a morsel more to tell of the Maendler story. In the middle 1990s the phone rang for me in my workshop in Preston: "Could I speak to Mr. McAllister please, it's Reginald Ellery speaking?" I gave a palpable shudder! "I'm sorry," I said, "but the only Reginald Ellery I know of, was the husband of Mancell Kirby, the harpsichordist." "That's right," said the voice, "I am his grandson." I intoned my relief with an audible sigh: "Jolly good, what can I do for you?"

It was the familiar saga of elderly folk becoming asset rich and cash poor and would I be good enough to do a valuation of Mancell's

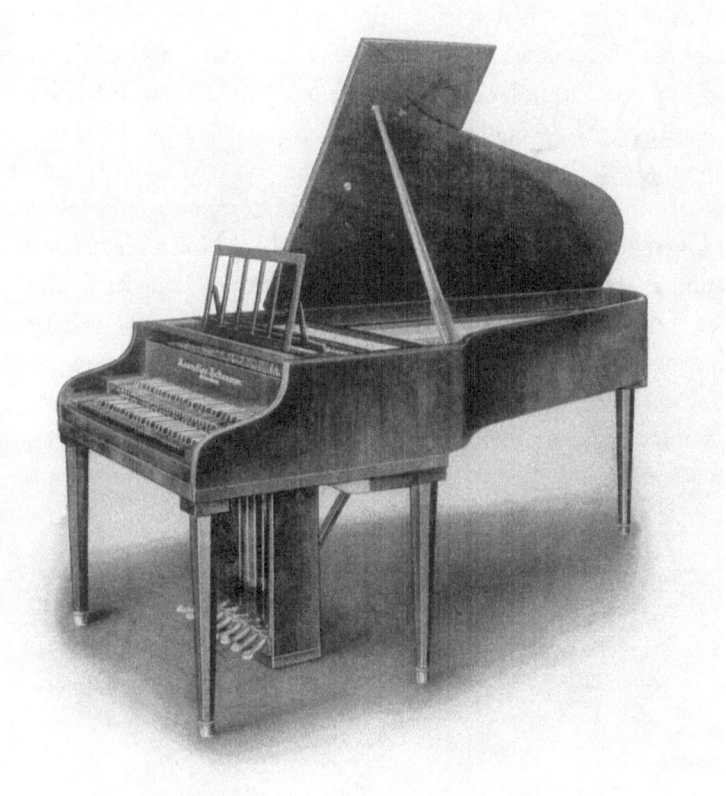

*Maendler-Schramm Model 246-8 with 16' and sustaining pedal: the
model owned by Mancell Kirby*

instruments, as the family was seeking to place her in an aged care facility. (Some people prefer to call them old folk's homes, though what's in a name? Growing old is altogether an unsophisticated business, and Mancell died in her hundredth year). As requested, I valued the instruments. In addition to the Maendler, there was a 1956 Dolmetsch concert grand and an Alec Hodsdon Virginals. I offered to buy the Maendler, prior to auction, partly because I suspected that no-one else would be interested, and too because of its historical significance. The family said thanks, but no thanks, as it had been determined that the instruments should go to auction! How could I forget? There it was, Lot 176, and purchased for a very reasonable sum; three people were interested, two carrying on the bidding to leave me well out of the equation. As noted above, the instrument has now been taken out of the country – conclusive proof that no one deserves to be lucky all the time.

BALLOONING ACQUAINTANCES

Should auld acquaintance be forgot, and
auld lang syne? – Robert Burns

Mars McMillan is one of those folk who on first meeting may impress as quiet and retiring but on better acquaintance proves to be surprisingly bold, someone who seems destined to 'make their mark.' A multifaceted talent, Mars is also a wonderful artist with an unerringly brilliant sense of colour and style, and could yet become more widely known for her work in paints alone. She could just as successfully have decided to be a cartoonist. With a knowledge of language refined to a nicety, she always claimed tackling *The Shorter Oxford Dictionary* for light reading, but finally gave it away "because the subject matter always kept changing." A great wit and a no-nonsense lady, Mars was once complimented at a concert, on the sheepskin she wore draped elegantly around her shoulders, her rejoinder: "Très sheep!"

Mars's woodwork is a joy to behold, clearly well thought out and deftly executed, indeed it sets a standard that I still aspire to! The instruments she has made are treasured by their owners, so what more need one say?

It was through Richard Ireland that I met recorder maker, the late Frederick Morgan. In those days he was not yet internationally famous as a great maker, but in addition to his making, he was also a wonderful player, and I undertook to organise a series of concerts for him (and Richard Ireland, harpsichord) in the rooms of the British Musical Society, East Melbourne, and the Presbyterian Church, Assembly Hall, Collins St. Melbourne. For some time Mars provided workshop space, gratis, to help Fred with his instrument making. He was a large and powerfully built man, and I remember Mars had purchased a cast iron 'fly press' for use in register making, and we were positioning planks so as to 'walk' it down from the back of my station wagon, when Fred arrived and simply picked it up and carried it inside, unassisted. The press must have tipped the scales at well over 100 kilos!

Fred was a meticulous craftsman whose work I much admired, prompting me to order two treble and two descant recorders from him. After measuring the bores of several instruments in Paris he asserted that French baroque pitch was "definitely" a′ = 415 Hz. At the time I had no reason to doubt his findings, however, some years later Fred remeasured the same instruments and came up with a′ = 409 Hz. Over the years the bores had shrunk unevenly so that they had become oval, and in the first instance he had measured the smaller dimension. Then later, realising his error, he measured the larger dimension. The conclusion that Fred came to, that of a′ = 409 Hz, we shall have reason to consider again. After Fred removed himself and his family to rural Victoria, meetings seemed to happen but by chance, and I did not see him for a number of years before his untimely demise, alas, in a car accident at the age of just 60.

It was under Fred's aegis that I met Jean-Louis Cocquillat, a harpsichord maker with many insights and good ideas. From the outset, his approach to building was perhaps more 'authentic' than some, which endeared him to Fred, and they shared a workshop together for some little while. I have met up with Jean-Louis again, in recent days, and it was great to realise that we still can find plenty to talk about.

One day I received a letter from Perth from a chap called Peter Kulessa, who was, he declared, nineteen years old, and wanted to become apprenticed. I wrote back saying that I was sorry, but I was not in a position to take on an apprentice, and then about one week later I received a phone call from Melbourne's Spencer Street (now Southern Cross) Railway Station, announcing his arrival! Such keenness! Mars, with unfailing generosity, found him a room and we all became good friends. Peter, who has a flair for working in both wood and metal, made a number of jigs and tools, and materially helped both Mars and myself. He had worked for sometime with

Perth organ builder John Larner, and boy, could he sharpen a plane blade!

It was an instrument after Dulcken he and I were making; I'd come to work early one morning and was admiring Peter's handiwork, when I noticed something odd about a tiny knot hole in the spine liner. Closer inspection revealed a neatly rolled scrap of paper, less than a half inch square when opened, which I fished out, unrolled, and read in the most minute Peter lettering: "Ha, Ha, you'll never find me." He never has disclosed whether he was glad or not that I had made the discovery. Peter shared with me, and a surprisingly large number of other instrument makers, a fascination for steam power and railways generally, and more recently he has volunteered his free time to the Puffing Billy Preservation Society, in the Dandenong Ranges outside Melbourne. Thanks for all the fun times, Pete, in the past and doubtless to come.

Another enthusiast friend to work with Mars and myself was one Andrew Bernard, a warm hearted and good-natured human being who had studied mathematics at the Australian National University, in Canberra. The tragedy for Andrew was that working with wood caused him great trauma with hay fever and allergies but he persevered to complete a magnificent Hass clavichord, decorated with hand sawn olive wood veneer, tortoiseshell naturals, ivory topped sharps (the ivory carefully salvaged from a disused piano keyboard), and so on. Possessed of a formidable intelligence, Andrew did much work in the IT Industry as a computer architect, but we still see him regularly, and we shall meet him again a little later as essential to these ramblings.

Over several years, Richard Schaumlöffel, an established builder in Adelaide, came to visit Mars et al, and, subsequently, ventured to spend some months working with me, in particular on a five and a half octave Schudi and Broadwood. This instrument now forms part of the important keyboard instrument collection of Dr. Ralph Schureck, in Sydney. I had decided that this harpsichord was to be based on the 1770 instrument at Fenton House, Hampstead, UK, essentially because the Schudi had been made prior to Broadwood's redesign of the plucking points that were made according to the suggestions of Dr. Gray of the British Museum, and hence was a model that largely predated most of the ever increasing influence being dumped on the harpsichord via the insidious creep of the new piano technology. Even so, the original instrument was provided with pedals that operated a Venetian Swell and Machine Stop, but the heart of the design was faithful to that of Schudi's Master, Hermanus Tabel. Richard has an enquiring mind, a surprisingly acerbic wit and is something of a traditionalist, so, for example, the case joints on the Schudi had to be dovetailed, not because they 'had' to be, but because that was how it was done originally by Schudi, and therefore, should be. I baulked at the idea of hand sawing dovetails to fit at obscure angles, so Richard took over and cut them beautifully! It is by appreciation of such actions, I fancy, that friendships are formed and cemented. The time came, however, over an entirely different matter, when apparently (though unwittingly, as is my fashion), I overstepped the dissent barrier with such dogmatic zeal that Richard shut down any interaction for a number of years. For me, it was clearly *Les Barricades Misterieuses*! So it is pleasing to record that, as of writing, our predestined coexistence has regained robust good health.

Marc Nobel is yet another talented instrument maker and one who established a workshop across the road from Mars. Aside from his making a horde of happy harpsichords, he and I have had many lively and friendship testing discussions, about all and sundry, and harpsichords as well. For some little time Marc has been specialising in the decoration of instruments, not just the harpsichord family but also the organ, about which instrument he is a considerable authority. At time of this writing (2010) he is building a sumptuous Italian organ with five ranks of pipes. A beautiful creation indeed!

For sheer elegance of execution, Marc's decorative work, in the style of the old masters, can hardly be exceeded and 'the word' about his work on organs has had him invited to execute commissions overseas. Together we have been to the United States and Europe to 'soak up the vibes' that only an inspection of the original instruments can offer.

One year, Marc and I were met at Brugge by Alan Todd, for the Festival of Flanders and its harpsichord exposition. An Aberdonian, (you can tell by his accent!), Alan is also a philosophy graduate and has worked and taught in a number of countries including Britain, Africa and New Zealand. Apparently he decided that he could do much worse than make Australia home. He is, by his own promulgation, possessed of a magnificent pair of pins, though I am always surprised that he should be wanting me to notice. All one can do is laugh and agree, or agree and then laugh, which latter, for reasons best known to himself, he seems to find less to his fancy! Alan had made his first instrument before he met me, and we too, have worked together, learned together, as well as having travelled together. No-one could wish for a stronger ally or more agreeable friend. Unfortunately, his agrarian interests now preclude frequent visits to the city; perhaps he prefers singing to his sheep rather than travelling around to tune his splendid instruments.

All these good people, and others still, contributing their karma to the melting pot of knowledge, could, with the right optimism, create a 'source' from which might well up thoughts, ideas, and even perhaps some answers; and so it did prove to be.

PLAYING TALKS

Tickling the ivories is no laughing matter!

For me, the great joy on finishing a harpsichord is having it played to me by its new owner. I confess to spending many hours keenly attentive to the performer's every reaction. Having attempted the violin as a callow youth it was clear that a keyboard performing career was not for me, so I have leeched the information I needed from the players for whom I was lucky enough to make instruments.

My very good friend, Roger Heagney, was a principal target in this respect and I would express a huge thanks to him for his seemingly endless patience. Sometimes sitting, sometimes kneeling, there I'd be, constantly questioning passages of florid finger work: "was that you or the instrument?" It must have driven him mad. But the process taught me the limitations of my instrument's action and where there was room for improvement from it or me. Roger, of course, is a wonderful player possessed of both a superb technical ability and an insightful musicianship. I listened and learned a lot and, hopefully, am still learning!

Over the years, Roger and I have done quite a deal of travelling together including a European and American harpsichord crawl and another taking Richard Ireland's Italian harpsichord, his Opus 1, on tour through China. More than anything, Roger is impressed by good musicianship and I recall that we were both completely won over by the harpist, Osian Ellis in concert in Oxford; it clearly didn't have to be a keyboard instrument to affect us. The qualities of Roger's sense of appreciation are no doubt what has led to the widest admiration of his playing and teaching, and not to forget his compositional works, which number many, and which have been conceived from a wonderfully broad palette.

In addition, there's his Irish humour, often leaving me flat footed, as on one occasion, page turning for him at a Christmas Midnight Mass, I asked him, (humbly), if I should stand for the Blessing? "No, no," he replied, "You surely don't want to ruin your image!" (And this to me, a son of the clergy.)

Talking of page turning: Richard Ireland was playing the 5th Brandenburg Concerto at a Christ Church South Yarra, Bach Festival. As I leaned forward to effect the turn, the page inexplicably found its way under my fingernail, and the music shot off the desk whacking the viola player fair in the back of the neck. Her reaction was more of a swine's grunt than a dog's Bach. [sic] Richard elegantly retrieved the music and played on, seemingly unruffled.

How could I forget page turning for Harold Fabrikant who was invited to play the Bach Concerto in D Minor, (and the Poulenc) before a live audience for the ABC, in Hobart, and the ABC, declaring a thorough search of Hobart town could produce no willing page turner, eventually persuaded me. I was there with only the clothes of a technician so I was pointed in the direction of a suit hire establishment and decked out in a brown velvet suit, yellow shirt, and staggeringly bright purple tie. Nobody would notice my 'desert' boots. Rehearsal time saw the conductor take the first movement of the Bach ridiculously fast for my taste. Harold remained imperturbable. At one point a halt was called to speak to the violas, at which juncture the page turner put up his hand and announced that every time the orchestra came in at the tutti, they pushed the beat. I could feel the hesitation, followed by the scathing glance and then the quintessentially British response: "Having said that, would you kindly say nothing further!" "Right you are," I said, with an exaggerated gesture of hand to forelock. But it was obvious that I needed to square off, so later, in the greenroom I engaged him with: "I'm sorry if I stepped into your territory earlier." "Yes you did!" "Well, I've apologised, I hope you're going to accept it?" "Yes I do!" "Mind you, I was right you know!" "Yes you were!" I rapidly sidled off feeling that I had, as we say, 'got away with it.'

New Zealander, Anthony Jennings first came to Australia on a Musica Viva tour. He played my double manual, originally based on Goujon but which somehow finished up with a cut through lute stop. (Mars called it 'the English Channel' model). I made my first Christian Zell copy for Tony, which I dispatched across the Tasman. Unfortunately, there was a freight-handlers' strike happening at Auckland airport, and the poor old harpsichord was literally left outside for ten days, hail, rain and shine. When it finally arrived for Tony to unpack, he discovered there was a centimetre or so of water sloshing around in the keywell. The water was mopped up and, apart from a few sticking jack tongues, nothing else seemed amiss. The sticking jacks were dried in the oven and away she went. Modified melamine resin glue is definitely waterproof! In due course, when Tony came to live permanently in Australia, I made him an Italian, after Trasuntino. Many times he played in Melbourne, the last being an afternoon and evening blockbuster performance of the complete English Suites of Bach. He always seemed such a relaxed player that Andrew Bernard suggested flying foxes should be mounted in the performance venues so that supporters could sling down grapes, Fantails (chewy, chocolate coated caramels) or other titbits to help sustain energy and ego. Tony was a gold medal student in Belgium, something of a star performer, and equally skilled at organ and harpsichord. He had a curiously strong finger technique and instruments always sounded louder after he had played them. At just fifty years of age, he died far too young!

At the time of Tony's death I was making him a German double after Johann Heinrich Harrass, of Grossbreitenbach. This instrument had been recommended to me, as something special, by the Swiss harpsichordist, the late Christiane Jaccottet. Like Tony, Christiane was also a wonderful musician, but I suspect she was somewhat underestimated as a performer. As a teacher, however, she enjoyed her students' reverence and affection, which I know made her heart glad. She was the top prize winner at the first Brugge Concours Clavecimbel in 1965, and subsequently served on the jury in 1974 and 1977. Some may find the playing on her many recordings a little dry, but this was manifestly not so in live performance. She was perhaps unlucky not to have been recorded by the folk at 'Telefunken

Royal Sound Stereo.' At the end of a solo recital for the Melbourne International Festival of Organ and Harpsichord, she played the 27th *Ordre* of François Couperin. I was mesmerised by her performance of *Les Pavots*. Afterwards, I said to her that her performance had not reminded me, in the slightest, of Wilfrid Mellors's description of 'The Poppies,' waving fussily in the breeze, in the middle of a field, but rather something more, and that her playing had left me deeply moved. She replied that one should remember that, throughout his life, Couperin had never enjoyed robust health and, as he aged, she was persuaded that he alleviated his pain and suffering by visiting the opium dens. "But" she said, "one cannot write this, because there is no proof." Recalling her performance, her artistry did, indeed, conjure up the excessively melancholic atmosphere of a haunt, wherein a myriad pipes and their insistent smokers, puffed out their sickly sweet fumes, cloying, dizzying, and all pervasive. Christiane's insight had enabled a transformation of the character of the piece and a performance so convincing, that it will remain for all my time, 'proof' enough for me!

Peter Watchorn, a long-time harpsichord enthusiast and old friend, is known widely as both builder and player. Now an expatriate living in Boston, on one of his all to infrequent visits home he made the acquaintance of the Harrass I had started making for Tony Jennings. Peter was also an admirer of Tony's playing, and the instrument and the circumstances must have touched a chord. He determined it was to be his, and so, after more than two years on the work bench, it was eventually finished and Peter gave its debut recital in the Melbourne International Festival of Organ and Harpsichord. Peter has made some splendid recordings on this instrument, including all the Bach Toccatas and the complete Concerto arrangements, after various masters, the Two and Three Part Inventions and, in 2010, Book Two of the WTC. The sound of the Harrass harpsichord on these discs represents the nearest I have achieved to my 'dream' sound, and I believe that Peter is happy too. He has suggested an even larger instrument, with a 16' register;

the challenge for the maker being to ensure the addition of the 16′ register does not destroy the 2×8′, 1×4′ tonal palette of the Harrass. I believe it can be done!

Peter, like me, is on something of a mission, to demystify the rather sad misconceptions that continue to hover, aura-like, around original instruments and which need to be expunged from the thought processes of both builders and performers. We take the view that one must give credit where credit is due and learn what one can from the best of the surviving examples and, of course, carefully preserve them for future generations to examine and coo over, but let there not be any pretence that their makers were something approaching demigods. There is some small evidence to suggest that the latest thinking of the boffins may be leading in this direction.

Could this be one of the reasons that motivated Leonhardt and Skowroneck, more than twenty five years ago, to perpetrate their mammoth hoax with the faking of a French harpsichord which they purported to be the work of Nicholas Lefebvre, 1755? If so, I suspect they had a good laugh, behind closed doors! Doubtless, they were not trying to emulate the duplicity of the unscrupulous nineteenth century dealer Leopoldo Francolini, though by default, of course, they did. Perhaps they simply lost patience with the persistent fawning of the masses and wanted to give them the finger. Again, it may have been the Leonhardt way of avoiding any criticism for his continuing support for one particular modern maker, though he did have his Rubios to dispel any such myth. Whatever the rationale it can only be seen as an ill-considered stunt, fooling some of the people for some of the time but not everybody for all time! I admit to being tempted to ask Uncle Gus what, after twenty odd years, prompted him to confess; didn't he think it was a good enough fake for him to take the secret to his grave?

Remy Gug apparently took the truth about his half dozen fakes to his grave! Skowroneck's book, *Cembalobau*, which was published post Leonhardt's public exposé, gives the reader a strong sense of its author's integrity but it makes no mention of the scam which has been for many, and I have to include myself, more than a little disconcerting! Be that as it may, the matter probably does not merit any further discussion, but it remains sufficiently outrageous not to be forgotten!

Besides, I have been fortunate that players have readily engaged my ears via their voices and fingers and, free of any obfuscation or subterfuge have, perforce, contributed enormously to the making of instruments that have 'good vibes.' A customer once said to me that if they liked the maker then it was a sure bet that they would like his instrument. One may presume that the reverse is true.

The conundrum is that both the maker and his instrument have to be 'approved of' by people who know nothing about the harpsichord, other than what they have read or heard, on radio or record. They may never have heard the player or the instrument in real life, but if the player is a 'big name' and the sounds they hear on record, appeal, these folk will speak forthrightly about all aspects of the product's musicality, without criticism; like a lot of sheep. Still others take heed!

Too many years ago, I remember being in San Francisco with Roger Heagney and doing a harpsichord 'crawl' with the distinguished maker, John Phillips. I have never forgotten the wonderful generosity of spirit exhibited by John, (whose instruments, incidentally, I think are wonderful), who spoke to us, in glowing terms, about a competitor's work. The maker was absent from the city at the time of our visit, so John had arranged a visitation to a private owner, ensuring that we were able to hear, see and play on his competitor's instrument, and so make our own assessment. Ten out of ten, sir!

Two other folk must be included in this exclusive set; the baroque cellist, Margaret Waugh, and mutual friend, violin maker, Warren Nolan-Fordham. Margaret played with Owen Watkins, recorder, and Peter Watchorn, harpsichord and later as principal cellist with Paul Dyer's Australian Brandenburg Orchestra. She is a wonderful musician, a fine keyboard player as well as cellist, and it was my privilege to make a five string cello for her, all from Australian timbers and which, I am gratified to say, she still plays. I was greatly assisted in achieving at least some of the subtleties of the task, by Warren, for the instrument was made in his workshop at Monsalvat, Victoria. I had persuaded myself that I would be doing no more than piano maker Cristofori had done when he made six cellos in the workshop of Stradivari, one of which, incidentally, just happens to reside in Australia. Warren and his wonderful work are well known to many: some regard him as a guru, though this, I fear me, is not to be encouraged! We have each been achieving in our separate workshops for the last several years, under the umbrella of a Community Co-operative Society called 'Worco.' Warren's shop was said to represent the Paris end!

THE FIRST UNISON

The First shall be Last and the Last shall be First

It has always seemed both frustrating and not a little odd to me that the final flowering of the English harpsichord resulted in the disposition of their actions being at variance to the great majority of their Continental counterparts; that perhaps this was one reason that their design has been so poorly represented as a model for present day makers to reproduce. Was it simply that their dogleg jacks, always plucking to the bass, gave the regular inclusion of the close plucking 'lute' stop, a little more room for the on-off movement of the register, and enabled the plectra of their lute and dogleg jacks to 'reach' over the offset 4' strings for their pluck? Perhaps: but Continental instruments by Dulcken and Hass, for example, still managed to retain their upper manual registers plucking to the right (i.e. towards the treble), whether constructed with lute stops or not, and then, in addition, there were those instruments that had their lute stops plucking to the left, yet with doglegs still plucking to the right, thus providing 2×8' on the upper manual. Why, too, did the later English builders invariably place the 4' register as their rearmost set of jacks? Yet more perplexing, there is evidence to suggest that later early English makers altered existing instruments to conform to the normality of their time, which quirkish behaviour jumped a hundred or so years and was still being perpetrated on unresisting instruments, well into the second half of the twentieth century (Rephann, *The Historical Harpsichord*, Vol. 4).

This chapter is concerned with the important issue of 'jack-turn' in historical instruments, and the implications this has for harpsichord design, voicing, and even playing.

Probably the best known example of jack-turn is the 1769 Taskin in The Russell Collection of Early Instruments at The University of Edinburgh, now, happily, restored to its original state. Reference to jack-turn will be met with again in my recording of the Pleyel restoration.

The Russell Collection holds a splendid harpsichord by Francis Coston, London, c. 1725. On the website of the Russell Collection Grant O'Brien gives conflicting information regarding the disposition of this instrument in his data sheet and a separate descriptive essay.

The website essay (Coston 2) gives the disposition of the registers of the Coston as:

Row 3	→	8′
Row 2	←	4′
Row 1	←	8′ dogleg

The website data sheet (Coston 3) records the disposition as:

Back Row	←	8′
Middle Row	←	4′
Front Row	→	8′ dogleg

An earlier O'Brien description in The Galpin Society Journal, (Coston 1, 7) records:

Row 3	←	8′
Row 2	←	4′
Row 1	→	8′ dogleg

(It would appear that the first of these three examples is but a mistake of transcription by the typist: two mistakes in actuality).

Directly after providing the first example, above, O'Brien goes on to record:

On the back of the removable nameboard there is the following instruction: 'The first unison speaks to the treble. The octave in the middle speaks to the base [sic].'

O'Brien suggests this instruction:

> ...presumably refers to the present set of 1761 jacks, in their present locations. But because of the cut of the dogleg in the near row of jacks, the 'first unison' (row 1) must pluck to the right and therefore towards the treble.

However, the first disposition diagram above suggests that, in the present arrangement, the dogleg jacks pluck to the left (to the bass), and this is patently not the case.

There is, of course, no proof that the nameboard instructives were written in 1761: it is possible, for example, that the refurbishment workers were simply being warned not to ignore what was an earlier record, (possibly that of the original maker himself or mayhap an owner from an earlier time?) not to alter the disposition to parallel those of the instruments of other (London?) makers whose practices were just beginning to influence musicians expectations of coming times. A little prophetic perhaps? Whoever the writer, the intended meaning of 'first unison' could just as conceivably have been O'Brien's row 3, (1st example), but the jacks were, in fact, not made in the well known, current (1761) fashion of dogleg plucking to the left, and, clearly, the dogleg jacks can't be about faced (jack-turned) as can those from an instrument constructed with short upper manual jacks and shove coupler disposition. The placement of the 4' register between the two 8's, supports the thought that we should be considering the Coston disposition, as originally built, as being rather more Continental (Flemish) than English, the one musical exception to this contention perhaps being the provision of the dogleg jacks instead of a manual coupler. To recognise, and thereafter ignore, the typographical error helps support this suspicion, while making no claim that dogleg jacks were, in any event, exclusively English.

It is possible, also, to suggest that the instructive was written by a third party, just prior to the remake, to remind the 1761 workers that the disposition of this instrument did not conform to what had, by then, evolved as common English practice, and, because doglegs were involved, to make sure that the jacks they made emulated the format of the originals. However, I choose not to be persuaded that this was the actual scenario.

Why don't writers about the harpsichord make at least some attempt to reach a consensus about appropriate terminology? In describing dispositions we have; short 8' and long 8', or front 8' and back 8', or upper 8' and lower 8', followed by plucking to the right and plucking to the left, or 'up-looking' 8' and 'down-looking' 8' or 'plucking to the treble' and 'plucking to the bass;' and so the list goes on! Now, on the Coston's nameboard, we encounter, 'the first unison speaks to the treble.' The precise meaning of this expression is not as defining as we might wish. Simplistically, 'first' could be understood to mean the row of 8' jacks closest to the player, or, as in post Tabel English instruments, the middle row between 8' and 4', as the 8' jack exclusively on the first or main manual. Alternatively, it could suggest the first in musical importance of two, or more than two, so that, unwittingly or intentionally, the maker Coston, or whoever wrote it, recorded for posterity, his understanding of the accepted harpsichord disposition which prevailed in the England of the pre 1720s, (pre Tabel). That is to say, the shorter 8' string sound quality, where the string on being plucked was pushed into the nut pin, was the 'first' or 'most sought after' or 'preferred' sound. Indeed, in an unaltered Ruckers, it was the only sound available from their instruments before the later inclusion of a second 8' string. When a choice of 8' stops was becoming more common, from the second half of the seventeenth century, then the shorter string might be described as 'first,' meaning first in matter of importance, (or perhaps even first in terms of its date of earliest use). I hesitate to borrow organ terminology but the organ builders' choice of 'principal' or 'diapason' perhaps best suggests this importance. I believe that, in reference to the string being plucked *into* its nut pin, there are a number of indicators to suggest 'first of importance' or 'principal' being the case description, and some discussion may be useful. What can be said with obvious certainty is that, prior to the inclusion of the second 8′ string, there was no necessity for any title or differentiation.

Ruckers harpsichords, doubles or singles, were provided, almost invariably, with only one 8′ string and one 4′ string, and the 8′ string was always plucked to the right, 'into the pin,' towards the right hand cheek piece. However, and not surprisingly, there is an exception to any rule, and an instrument that I have examined closely, (in private ownership in the USA), appears, conclusively, to have been originally constructed as a single manual with 2×8′, 1×4′ strings. To my knowledge, all Ruckers instruments had their 4′ strings laid out so that they were plucked by jacks facing to the left, that is, towards the bass; so too this instrument, with its 4′ scaling being half that of the shorter 8′ string; front 8′ plucking to the right.

If one considers the Ruckers's 1×8′, 1×4′ design it becomes apparent that any of the following arrangements were available for them to choose from:

1.	8 ←	4 ←
2.	8 ←	4 →
3.	8 →	4 →
4.	8 →	4 ←

After little thought we may discount numbers 1 and 3 for simple constructional reasons, (for this realisation we have to wear our sixteenth century hats), but there is clearly more likelihood of damper interference, which is otherwise more readily avoided. On the other hand, number 2 seems to have some merit, particularly in relation to the high treble area of the 4′ because there the 4′ strings are just that little bit shorter, which could prove to be an important consideration in a double manual where they were expected to span an action gap containing the Ruckers standard four registers. Examples of this 'shorter 4′ syndrome' may be seen in the work of a number of twentieth century makers, though these modern makers manifestly did not seek to have the scaling of their 4′ strings halve that of their shorter 8′ strings. It is obvious that the Ruckers definitely did attempt to provide a 4′ scale of half their 8′ scale for the top two octaves of their harpsichord's compass, and bearing this important point in mind, it suddenly becomes clear that the 4′ bridge (not the nut, for it would then encroach on the 4′ tuning pins) would have to be moved to a position on the soundboard where it would begin to cramp the free soundboard area of the 8′ bridge. Bingo, and we are left with disposition number 4! It is also important to realise that Ruckers were designing 8′ harpsichords to which was added a 4′ as the 'cream on the cake,' and not the reverse; that is, the emphasis is the 4′ scaling is half that of the 8′ and not that, though it necessarily is so, the 8′ scaling is twice that of the 4′.

On careful examination of any harpsichord, it will be clear that the plucking action of the plectrum pushing past the string, unseats the string from a wholly vertical motion to one where the pluck tends to initially push the string either into or away from the nut and bridge pins, with the attendant result of an elliptical vibration of the string; the greatest freedom of vibration ('bloom') being obtained when the string is pushed by the pluck away from its pin. As discussed above, it is clear that either option was available to the Ruckers, but it seems the bloom we hear from strings being plucked away from their pins was not the sound that was sought after by Ruckers nor, indeed, their customers, yet this characteristic bloom, if observed in the 4′ register was, perhaps, accepted as a spicy complement to the ensemble. The biggest problem associated with the 4′ strings being plucked to the left is the very acute angle the string takes as it leaves the nut pin to the tuning-pin and this was, doubtless, a contributing factor in Ruckers making their 4' tuning pins of smaller diameter, and not simply just for ease of tuning.

In the first quarter of the eighteenth century, Francis Coston would have had no reason not to follow existing Ruckers type examples. Nevertheless, this acute angle of 4' string from nut to tuning pin was, perhaps, reason enough (in 1761), for the restorer to bring sixteen treble strings through holes drilled in the 8' nut where, because of the closeness of the 4' tuning pins to the 4' nut, the acuteness of the angle is most pronounced. It could hardly be considered essential though, because the Coston harpsichord does not have a cut through lute register, like later Kirckmans, or Schudis, and so on. It is possible that the treble 4' strings in English instruments such as Kirckman and Schudi and others, instead of exhibiting too much side-draught, actually demonstrate too little. One solution is to have the 4' string passing through the 8' nut but with side-draught to the left, rather than the right. This also has the added bonus of completely freeing the space available for the inclusion of a lute register, if such a stop is desired, for now the angle of side-draught of the 4' strings is accommodated under the semitone apart, or close paired, 8' strings. Again, this is not something new, for a number of twentieth century makers have adopted this concept, including me, and I am bound to say that it makes little observable difference in tone quality to that of a normally laid out 4' string band; and certainly no perceptibly less bloom.

It hardly needs to be observed that eighteenth century French and English, and to a slightly lesser extent, German, instruments are all based on Ruckers, yet the disposition of the post-Tabel English harpsichords stand apart because their dogleg jacks pluck the longer 8' strings. If we consider that the shorter 8' string is the principal sound then it made sense for the later English makers to place their 4' register furthermost from the player, in effect maintaining Ruckers 8'+4' combination but moving it in both practicality and importance from the Ruckers's upper manual to the (post Tabel) lower manual. As O'Brien has pointed out, the Ruckers also made a few of what he describes as an export 'French' model, with an extended bass, where the 'principal' manual was the lower, with the transposition of a fourth available on the upper manual. Examples of this export model doubtless also found their way to England where, as we know, the musicians had long expected instruments with larger bass compasses, and just such an example may well have been observed by Tabel and his pupils. It suggests that later English instruments should be voiced, therefore, with this possibility in mind.

I believe it is reasonable to suggest that, (if actually inscribed by him), Coston's 'first unison' was in fact his 'principal' voice, equivalent to the only Ruckers 8′ string, which was the one that was being plucked to the right, available on the upper manual, the manual, on the vast majority of Ruckers's doubles, for playing at standard pitch. This has clear implications for both voicing and stagger, particularly in later, more complicated instruments, as will be realised. However, the fact is that the original jacks in the Coston instrument have not survived, those presently in the instrument date from the 1761 rebuild, and hence, like many of these conundrums, the unequivocal outcome of the maker's original voicing and set-up, indeed, the effective realization of an 'instruction to himself,' must remain impossible to prove.

An instrument by Joseph Mahoon, dated 1738, may be observed to retain its original dogleg jacks and they, too, pluck the shorter 8′ string, while its lute register jacks pluck the longer 8′ string. Such arrangement is by no means unique and offers the possibility of 2×8′ on the upper manual (Hubbard).

These machinations must influence voicing, as it slowly dawns that the 'unison of first importance,' the 'principal' voice, should not be voiced as subservient to its partner. This is not to say that one is precluded from voicing the upper manual 8′ of a French double more gently than that of its lower manual 8′, for if ever such a concept applied to any instrument's voicing it is surely that of a late French double. But a German or Flemish double, or a Francis Coston? Perhaps not, and suddenly, having attempted this bold outcome, we will come to hear with new ears, particularly the music of Bach; and who greater a composer to warrant such a premium result? For me, the 'Modern French Double,' with 'French' voicing, presents at its least effective in playing Bach, when all of a sudden it can appear to be just a little too luxurious and well mannered, almost too representative of the opulence of the late eighteenth century.

Meanwhile, we are constrained to recognise the truth of the Biblical saying 'the First shall be Last and the Last shall be First;' when the First register by date of conception and use, shall be the Last voice to be heard by the listener, or if preferred the Last 'sound quality' to reach the ear of the hearer should be the messenger of 'good taste,' or arbiter elegantiarum, the First of greatest importance. To our huge delight, the plucking order of the registers conspires to point up such an outcome, for nothing more is required from them but to be in harmony with the action's 'natural' plucking order, as dictated by the motion of the keys, the which continue their stance of remaining silent, but seemingly knowing, levers. Of course, the 4' register, having been voiced rather more gently, shall always speak first.

CATNAP ONE

Britannica's cats

In 1979 Encyclopaedia Britannica Inc., Chicago, published a replica, in facsimile, of the first edition of the three volume Britannica, dated 1768. Immediately, it became imperative that I acquire a copy! The original Britannica which had been compiled by three canny Scots from Edinburgh, was made available by subscription only, and then in instalments, making complete 200 year old copies, best suited to photograph for facsimile, difficult to find. However, find one they did and my copy rewarded me with many delights to be savoured from between its covers. It will be remembered that the original publication predated, by twenty years, the first British convict settlement of Botany Bay, in present day New South Wales.

Recorded under the genus *Felis*, [sic] this particular entry provides general descriptions (as then known) of the larger members of the cat family and then we discover, under item number seven, a description of the common domestic cat. Follows a slightly abridged version, but sufficient, I trust, that we may share the editor's ease with, and an obvious enjoyment of, the English language:

> The cat is a well known domestic animal and therefore requires no particular description.
>
> Of all domestic animals, the character of the cat is the most equivocal and suspicious. He is kept, not for any amiable qualities, but purely with a view to banish rats and mice and other noxious animals from our houses, graneries etc. Although cats, when young, are playful and gay, they possess at the same time an innate malice and perverse disposition, which increases as they grow up, and which education learns them to conceal but never to subdue. Constantly bent upon theft and rapine,

though in a domestic state, they are full of cunning and dissimulation; they conceal all their designs; seize every opportunity of doing mischief, and then fly from punishment. They easily take on the habits of society, but never its manners; for they have only the appearance of friendship and attachment. This disangenuity [sic] of character is betrayed by the obliquity of their movements and the ambiguity of their looks. In a word, the cat is totally destitute of friendship; he thinks and acts for himself alone. He loves ease, and searches for the softest and warmest places to repose himself. The cat is likewise very amorous; and, which is very singular, the female is more ardent than the male; she not only invites, but searches after and calls upon him to satisfy the fury of her desires; and if the male disdains or flies from her, she pursues, bites, and in a manner compels him.

The cat is incapable of restraint and consequently of being educated to any extent. However, we are told that the Greeks in the island of Cyprus trained this animal to catch and devour serpents, with which the island was greatly infested. This, however, was not the effect of obedience, but of a general taste for slaughter; for he delights in watching, attacking, and destroying all kinds of weak animals indifferently. After he has caught them, he sports with them and torments them a long time, and at last kills them (when his belly is full) purely to gratify his sanguinary appetite.

Cats take about eighteen months before they come to their full growth; but they are capable of propagation in twelve months, and retain this facility all their life. They eat slowly and are peculiarly fond of fishes. They walk softly and without making any noise. They drink frequently; their sleep is light; and they often assume the appearance of sleeping, when in reality they are meditating mischief.

Clearly, any searches in this Britannica for entries such as 'kangaroo' or 'wombat' and so on, are doomed to failure, though you will find an extensive article on farriery, and this surely warranted because the horse then represented the power source that constituted the most efficient, indeed only, means of overland transportation, besides of course, one's own legs, before the introduction of railways and steam power.

Meanwhile, there should be a plebiscite taken of those who claim no empathy with cats! I work in a Co-operative that is proudly patronized by a haughty desexed female – a superbly marked, and quite rare ginger tabby called Ted – short for adopted!

'Resistance is Futile...'

PITCH AND SCALING

Which pitch is which?

The first attempted draft of this chapter was written in 1989, whilst I was in Boston visiting Peter Watchorn, and one evening after an entertaining dinner with the late Howard Schott, I was bold enough to seek from him an encouraging response. Since that time, useful work on scalings and pitch has been achieved by a number of eminent makers, and yet nothing that I have read to date has had quite the same slant nor arrived at such a pragmatic conclusion. Nevertheless, I have maintained a confidence in the usefulness of this approach and, therefore, feel it is worthwhile promulgating. This chapter then, is the original article, essentially verbatim, though updated and corrected for error.

Firstly, I must give much credit to Andrew Bernard to whom I had shown an article in The Diapason Magazine, on harpsichord maker E. O. Wit. Therein, Wit recorded that he scaled his instruments according to 'half wavelength' principles and Andrew made the quantum leap and did the maths necessary to establish a pitch for the 1769 Taskin. Peter Watchorn also offered much encouragement and assistance, especially with the first draft: thanks chaps.

The uncertainty surrounding the multiplicity of pitches that prevailed in the sixteenth, seventeenth, and eighteenth centuries continues to plague makers of reproduction stringed instruments into the twenty-first century. It is hoped to provide what might be described as a 'template' which may be overlaid on the string bands of original instruments to determine an appropriate pitch level relevant to the physical framework which has survived. The successful creation of what might be termed a pitch standard would enable ready comparisons to be made between the differing string lengths of surviving early instruments and their relationship to a definable pitch.

A pitch standard may be defined as an attempt, made at a particular time or place, to quantify the range of sounds, high to low, which are audible to the human ear, and to establish a particular frequency level within that range upon which organised patterns of notes may be based. While the range of sounds audible to the human ear may be assumed to have remained constant, the pitch standards chosen from within that range have varied considerably throughout the history of music. Nominally, these days, we employ two pitch standards; International Concert Pitch: $a' = 440$ Hz and a twentieth century approximation of 'old' pitch, one equal tempered semitone lower: $a' = 415.3$ Hz, whilst down to $a' = 392$ Hz and up to $a' = 465$ Hz are becoming ever more common in usage. The German physicist, Heinrich Hertz, [1857–1894], was responsible for the pioneering work of providing the possibility of a precise definition of pitch. Crucial to a full appreciation of the instruments of former times, is an understanding of the pitch standards for which they were designed.

In building their instruments, the earliest harpsichord makers had to contend with the fact that over and above the non-standardized pitches in common use, there also existed a number of nominal pitch standards. Choir pitch and Chamber pitch, for example, may be considered standards because they were a definable interval apart, chamber pitch being a fourth higher than choir pitch. Chor-ton and Cammer-ton, were often one whole tone apart, sometimes more. Fundamental to establishing the design pitch of any stringed instrument is the calculation of its 'scaling,' or the speaking length of its strings, and it seems reasonable to suggest that the earliest makers established their concepts of string scalings from the practices employed by early organ builders. These organ builders established the length of the lowest pipe on the organ keyboard, C, at a nominal eight feet, from which is derived the nomenclature of 16', 8', 4' and so on, to describe the pitch of the various ranks of pipes contained in an organ's specification. As well as the harpsichord, it follows that a piano may also be described as an instrument designed at 8' pitch, though use of this appellation is not to be seen in its descriptive literature. It should be clear that using copper alloy wire, as they did, the early harpsichord makers could not scale their c″ string length to mirror that of the speaking length of the corresponding c″ organ pipe. Copper alloy wire (what we usually call spring brass) will only stand being tuned to a pitch about one fourth lower than that pitch now understood as being applicable to an appropriate iron wire, a fact which may be determined by comparison of the relevant tensile strengths of the two materials.

That both choir and chamber pitch standards were being accommodated by the earliest harpsichord makers is reflected in the number of extant original instruments whose keyboards have top notes of either c‴ or f‴, when there is, in fact, little written music surviving from this early period which calls for notes higher than c‴. It is interesting to observe that if one aligns the string bands of a number of such instruments so that their nominal pitches agree, a remarkable similarity exists in their scaling concepts, particularly so when it is remembered that there existed, in those times, no absolute standard of pitch nor a precise method of establishing one. By the middle of the seventeenth century, however, as choir and chamber pitch fell out of use, short and longs scales began to give way to more standardised string lengths. Allowing then for the different pitch standards, of which Choir and Chamber were just two, Italian harpsichords, in particular, show remarkable scaling similarities, one to another, unchanged in principle over more than two hundred years. The great majority of these Italian harpsichords had two sets of strings, either 1×8′ and 1×4′, or later on, 2×8′, however, the point is that the brass strings were only required to span an action gap containing two registers of jacks. This is of greatest significance, for whilst makers continued to use only two sets of strings and jacks there was no requirement to change from brass stringing, a revision which otherwise would have been necessary as brass wire did not have the tensile strength to span a wider gap containing more registers as the keyboard range continued its upward climb.

Meanwhile, in the Low Countries, the Ruckers of Antwerp took an expansive approach from the common practice in Italy, and the harpsichord making Ruckers family members were to become legends in their own lifetimes. Were there hidden secrets to their success? Perhaps one was the fact that Ruckers offered their customers an instrument which incorporated both choir and chamber pitches in the one case. The Edinburgh University Ruckers transposing double harpsichord, dated 1638, is the classic, unaltered example and, like the early Italians, was provided with just two choirs of strings, 1×8′ and 1×4′. It is probable that this disposition reflected the importance which Ruckers (and the Italians) placed on string scaling, for it obviates having to consider the consequences of providing two sets of 8′ strings at the same pitch when they necessarily had different speaking lengths. This issue was addressed by other makers, to be seen, for example, with the use of separate nuts of each 8′ string (Italian, Yale), and 'offset' bridge pinning (Kirckman and others). Piano makers, of course, solved the dilemma by 'crenellating' their bridges, a solution which is simply not possible on the harpsichord. (Some early pianoforte makers bothered to crenellate only the speaking side of their bridges, for example, a piano by William Lavestaff, London, c. 1815, in the possession of the writer's daughter).

A second and more likely hypothesis is that Ruckers, either by default or design, succeeded in creating a new and sought-after sound, which, essentially, may be seen as the result of two factors:

Φ   A new scaling concept, necessitated by the fact that four registers of jacks now required an action gap of twice the usual width, and:

Φ   The resultant use of iron wire in the stringing (brass wire was still to be used for the low tenor and bass of the instrument). Iron has the necessary tensile strength to span the wider gap and, as was no doubt soon discovered, gives noticeably greater tuning stability than brass. While Van Blankenburg (1739) notes: "but since they (copper strings) do not sound as clear as iron ones in the treble, harpsichords are seldom made this way." (Hubbard, 73).

It was to compensate for the longer scales and hence greater tension (for a given pitch and for wire of the same diameter) that Ruckers made the case scantlings of their instruments to be of larger dimensions than their Italian relatives.

So, the use of iron rather than brass wire resulted in the creation of a new sound; a sound which literally took the harpsichord devotee world by storm; a sound which was lavishly praised and diligently copied by later makers. Indeed, just when Ruckers instruments might reasonably have been expected to have outlasted their usefulness, they were rebuilt, in many cases more than once; a practice particularly prevalent in France where it was known as *ravalement*. Ruckers had paid close attention to Pythagorean principles in the scalings of the trebles of their instruments, from middle C upwards, and it is in this 'just' area of the string band that we are interested today in establishing a pitch for the instrument, with its consequent important bearing on tone colour. That practical layout problems exist with regard to the total size of the case or the minimum length of the highest pitched string in the treble, is obvious enough, but these issues beg the question of how our ears choose to decipher the sounds produced in this just area of the compass.

For a moment, let us examine the legacy of some notable eighteenth century builders. In any discussion of harpsichord string scalings the work of the Parisian builder, Pascal Taskin, deserves special mention for a number of reasons:

Φ Taskin's own harpsichord, dated 1769, survives, and now forms part of the Russell Collection of early keyboard instruments at The University of Edinburgh.

Φ Taskin's tuning fork also survives at the Academy of Applied Sciences, Paris. This fork was measured by the nineteenth century French mathematician Lissajous as: $a' = 409$ Hz. (Helmholtz).

Φ The excellence of Taskin's work as a harpsichord maker was recognised in his own lifetime, and Gerber recorded his own understanding of Taskin's instruments as being 'mathematically correct in design' (Gerber).

In addition, the 1769 (Edinburgh) and 1770 (Yale) examples of Taskin's harpsichords have inspired more reproduction 'copies' than any other historic original. The excellent work of William Dowd (Schott, Vol. 1) sets out Taskin's design parameters. The scalings of these two instruments along with those of Taskin's mentor, Blanchet, clearly demonstrate that a scaling standard was being adhered to, for between the 1746 Blanchet and the 1770 Taskin, for instance, the scale variation at c'' is just one millimetre! (that is, five instruments in all).

In England, those most professional of makers, Kirckman and his competitor, Schudi, also produced instruments whose scalings were so similar that it seems clear that they too were working to a standard; one perhaps encouraged or dictated by their close competitive relationship. Schudi, of course, is reputed to have made a harpsichord for Handel, but whether the composer actually owned one or not we may safely assume he knew well the work of both builders, aside from his being a personal friend of Schudi. Handel's tuning fork has survived, pitch $a' = 422.5$ Hz. It is tantalising to consider that Handel may have purchased this fork from Schudi. Even if he had not, one need not be forgiven the notion that Schudi knew enough about his craft to ensure his instruments sounded their best, and functioned reliably, at the favourite pitch sought by the most famous musician in town.

It hardly needs to be stated that these early harpsichord makers had no quantified knowledge of physics or acoustics, but relied solely on the empirical method of trial and observation. The pitch standard expressed as a' = 440 Hz was not established until 1929, when it was chosen because it happened to be the frequency of the radio call signal of the BBC Home Service. (Grove 5).

Today the physics of a vibrating string should be well known to all instrument makers, but what does the theory of a string vibrating at half its wavelength in air show us about the string scalings of early harpsichords? The Encyclopaedia Britannica provides the definition:

When vibrating in its fundamental or first harmonic mode, a string vibrates as a whole in a single segment, passing through all bow-shaped curves from the extreme arc on one side of the equilibrium position to the extreme arc on the other side and back again in one complete cycle, or period, of motion. In this case the length of the string is one half the wavelength of the transverse wave running back and forth along the string.

The equation is given as:

$$\lambda = v / f$$

where
λ is wavelength
v is velocity
f is frequency

It is well known that the speed of sound varies when measured in air at different temperatures. Encyclopaedia Britannica states that the first attempt generally accepted today as offering any credibility of accuracy from a scientific standpoint, were experiments carried out in still air by the Academy of Applied Sciences, Paris in 1750. Calibrated to 0 °C the Academy calculated the speed of sound to be 332 m s^{-1}, a figure which was to vary by less than 1% over the next two centuries. The point, however, is that 332 m s^{-1} would have been the figure available to Pascal Taskin, the scaling of whose instruments seem to reflect some awareness of its relevance. Today, the speed of sound is accepted as 331.3 m s^{-1} at 0 °C.

0 °C is the temperature at which water turns to ice and along with the boiling point of water at 100 °C, were concepts which required no scientific instruments to be owned by early enquirers to enable them to achieve a definition of precision, for a temperature measurement scale, for those phenomena. The Swedish astronomer, Anders Celsius [1701–1744], read his defining paper to the Swedish Science Academy in 1742, which saw his name given to the scale. Anyhow, Paris was then, and is now, a cold capital and, of course, everyone is aware that a harpsichord sounds far better in cold conditions than in hot. So, armed with these simple expressions of understanding, we shall proceed.

From the above it can be seen that the equation for frequency is expressed:

$$f = v / \lambda$$

Now, let us apply this formula to the 1769 Taskin. Taskin's scaling for the short string is recorded by Dowd as c″ = 339 mm. This must be multiplied by two if the string speaks at 'half wavelength,' so the value we must use is 678 mm.

For the speed of sound in air, we take the established value of 330.56 m s^{-1} at 20 °C at up to 200 m above sea level.

Thus we have for the note c″:

$$f = 330.56 \text{ m s}^{-1} / .678 \text{ m} = 487 \text{ Hz}$$

We are interested in the frequency of a′ because we have Taskin's tuning fork for this pitch.

In equal temperament c″ is 523.3 Hz when a′ is 440 Hz. Using this ratio we calculate a′ to be:

$$a' = 487 \times 440 / 523.3 = 409 \text{ Hz}$$

In simple terms, this indicates that, when tuned to $a' = 409$ Hz, the 1769 Taskin has its just scaled strings speaking at 'half their wavelength.'

The following are some harpsichord scalings related by the half wavelength equation, to pitch. Where two 2×8' strings are present the length given, as in the Taskin, is that of the shorter 8' string. This short 8' string should be considered the fundamental resonating length in all altered instruments by Ruckers and all subsequent instruments based on the Ruckers design, particularly when, as practised by Ruckers, and others besides, the 4' scalings halve that of the instruments' shorter 8' scalings. Calculations give:

Instrument	Scale mm	Frequency a' Hz
Ruckers Double 1638	356	392
Moermans 1642	315	440
Schudi 1771	330	421
Hitchcock c. 1720	316	440
Taskin 1769	339	409
Hass 1734	344	405

Modern reproduction iron wire, such as Rose or Millers Falls, works perfectly well with the above scalings relative to the pitches assigned, the tension imposed on the wire not taking it too close to, or beyond, its elastic limit.

Grant O'Brien has argued comprehensively that Ruckers pitch for a' was between 413 Hz and 418 Hz, which he averages to 415 Hz, and describes this as his 'reference' pitch. This may be very useful in ascribing the relative pitches of other Ruckers instruments, however, the above table indicates that Ruckers reference pitch should be $a' = 392$ Hz, or one whole tone lower than $a' = 440$ Hz. O'Brien assessed his pitch standard by comparing the Ruckers's scaling (1638 being the unique unaltered Ruckers original) to that of the long string of the Taskin, but the comparison of apples with oranges can, as the adage itself suggests, create a false premise, and Taskin's 4′ scaling mirrors half the length of his shorter 8′ string length, not the longer.

So, what relevance the half wavelength factor? Apart from its importance in the comparison of pitches of unaltered original harpsichords it does seem to suggest that the best of the old makers employed a 'knowing' approach to scaling issues appropriate to prevailing pitch requirements, a position only rarely achieved by present day makers caught up, as they are, in the art of close or exact copying. Intriguingly, other historic stringed instrument makers also seemed to be Gnostic, or 'in the know.' Consider the long and short pattern Stradivari violins; the degree of scale shortening and Stradivari's timing of his introduction of the change. It is all very intriguing; but it is another story...

CATNAP ONE AND A HALF

A Kit Kat break

The following has nothing whatever to do with the half wavelength factor, but Plate XXX, of *Musical Instruments* by Karl Geiringer depicts the wonderfully detailed Allegory of Hearing by Jan Brueghel, 1618, from the Prado, Madrid. One should recognise the harpsichord in the painting as being by a member of the Ruckers family, and observe, importantly, its unaligned double keyboards, as well as the interior lid painting, the block printed keywell papers, and the marbling of the paintwork of the case with the register ends projecting through the cheekpiece in the traditional Ruckers manner. The whole is an important and spectacular painting and deserves our close critical scrutiny, along with examples of a similar scene by several other artists.

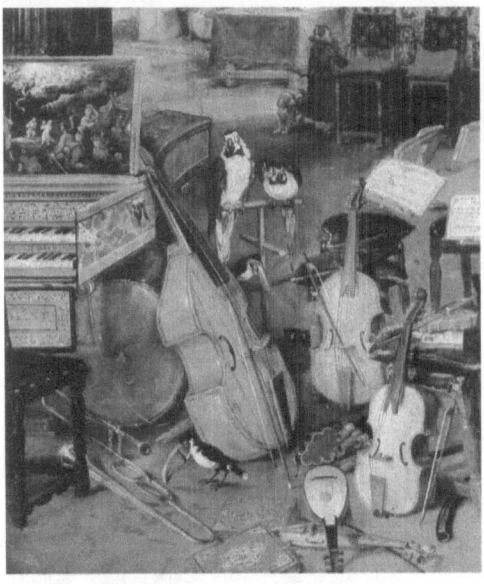

Detail of The Allegory of Hearing

TELLING TALES

Anecdote, n. 1. Secret, private, or hitherto
unpublished narratives or details of history

These titbits will doubtless reveal as much about me as they may about whom they are told; which is, indeed, only fair enough. So in no chronological order:

I have, since Paul Dyer's establishment of the Australian Brandenburg Orchestra, in 1989, been involved as their harpsichord tuner and general dogsbody. Gary Price was the Orchestra Manager at the time and we were asked to hire a three ton truck and take the harpsichords, cellos, double bass, clothes, 'set' items, and so on, down to Melbourne, to the Melbourne Club, (still men only, by the way; curious in these days of the, so called, equality of the sexes). As the Orchestra was appearing in Sydney and Melbourne on consecutive nights, Gary and I decided that we should leave immediately after the Sydney performance. Away we went... got as far as Kings Street, Newtown, (in central Sydney), somewhat after midnight, when suddenly we found ourselves surrounded by 5 police cars, sirens, men with guns, the works. "Out of the truck," etc, etc. I couldn't help myself and much to Gary's alarm, I declared: "This is an outrage, I'm from Victoria," to which the Sergeant bawled out: "Shut up!" Chastised and chastened, I immediately offered him a cigarette in mollification... Apparently there had been a report of a white truck heading out of town, carrying drugs. We had no drugs, and were not arrested – but neither was there any apology for the inconvenience – so I enjoined the officer to radio ahead and forewarn his fellows along the route, that we were coming through. I should report that the drive to Melbourne was thereafter without incident, for the ensuing discussion kept us both awake during the wee small hours, and as you might reasonably expect, no speed limits were exceeded.

The noted counter-tenor, Andreas Scholl, is not noted for his absent-mindedness, rather the opposite, but I have to tell that on one occasion, when singing for the 'Brandenburgers,' he left his concert shoes at the hotel and mine were the only ones that fitted him. Nobody in the audience seemed to notice that the harpsichord was being tuned by a man wearing only his socks, (on his feet, that is).

The late William Dowd, on one of his sojourns to France, found an apparently unaltered French harpsichord by Blanchet which still had some of its eighteenth century strings and jacks, with their quills, still in place. After carefully studying the action process it seemed to Dowd that the 4′ was staggered to speak last. Unable to accept this, Dowd experimented with the 4′ speaking second. The word spread round the harpsichord world like wild fire and many builders were trying it out. I recall one year in Brugge, engaging Reinhardt von Nagel, (Dowd's business partner at the time), with a friendly: "Okay Reinhardt, what's all this bullshit about your 4′ speaking second?" Inflating himself to his maximum height, he replied with an audible click of the heels: "I speak fluent French, German and English, I have no wish to speak Australian!" How did he know that I was from Australia? But it terminated the conversation! What he certainly did not know was that I had, some little time before, mentioned the subject of this 4′ speaking second stagger to Dowd who declared that he wished he had never made the claim, as it was musically naïve. Which leads fairly into the next snippet.

I was in New Zealand, visiting Tony Jennings, when he said that there was a lady who owned a copy of the late John Barnes's Dulcken single and would I be prepared to 'give it the once over' for her. It was a nicely made, 2×8′ single. As soon as I played it, it was clear that the speaking order of the registers was incorrect, the back 8′ speaking last. I had the greatest difficulty convincing the owner that it would revolutionise the instrument if I were to change the speaking order to front 8′ last, and I said that, as I would shortly be visiting John Barnes I would ask him to allow me to check out his original, and if I was incorrect I would change her instrument back to how it was, on my return (one of the advantages of adjusting screws on the bottom of the jacks, in this instance). Happily, having finished adjusting the instrument, she appreciated the change in its speech, and decided to be wholly convinced by the conception. Later, in Edinburgh, I did thoroughly check out John Barnes's Dulcken, only to find that it was impossible to prove, some notes were staggered one way, some the other. But, as I said, for me there is no question to answer; the shorter string, plucking to the right, should sound last in the plucking sequence.

Many amusing letters came from one Lothar (Joe) Sontag who lived in Weil am Rhine, on the Swiss border. In one he declared that it had been so hot of late that he and his wife, Anita, had to sleep under a "rotating ceiling propeller." We had met on an outback coach tour to the Alice and as I stepped from the bus, Joe had just put his pipe to his lips. "Oh," I said, "I love the smell of a good pipe!" He clicked his heels and replied: "Sank you for zuh compliment but I have not yet begun to light it." How could one respond to that?

Which, of course, reminds me of the dinner party at Peter Watchorn's home, in Boston, when we entertained the late Howard Schott. On leaving, we had moved to the veranda to say our good-byes, and I lit my first cigarette for the night. Howard looked up and observed: "Ah, you smoke tobacco, how very old fashioned," then turning, strode resolutely off, to vanish from sight in the darkness of the night. I have now given up the filthy habit!

Which somehow moves sequentially to the time Alan Todd, Marc Nobel, and I arrived at Peter Watchorn's apartment in Vienna, at two o'clock in the morning, only to discover that we had been locked out of our accommodation across the hallway, and the key was not to be found. In the end, five people in all finished up camping in Peter's one bedroom. I was desperately tired, fell into a deep sleep and immediately started snoring, and I mean snoring. I was woken time and again by prods, pillows and exhortations, in vain efforts to gain a little peace, but I could not stay awake. I moved to my knees, stuck fingers down my throat, and so on, all to no avail. Around four o'clock I was made acutely aware of just how parlous the situation had become when Peter bellowed at the top of his voice: "You bloody animal." That was followed by an absolute and embarrassed silence! I believe, by the way, that it may well have been the very first and only time I have heard Peter curse, for he is surely a man of measurable refinement.

In New Zealand again, Tony said that he had arranged a live broadcast on Radio NZ and hoped I wouldn't mind being part of it. So there we were, seated in the studio in front of our microphones and each with our glass of water before us on our little table. The man apparently gave some signal and Tony iterated that it was ten years since he had first visited Australia when he had been impressed by the harpsichords of a local maker, Alastair McAllister, who was with him now in the studio. "And I'd just like to ask you Alastair, what is it that makes you such a bloody great tit?" Stunned speechless, I was reaching desperately for my water, when the man in his booth said: "Cut it out Jennings! Now I'll have to rewind the tape"... I still don't believe I had ever done anything to merit such devilment!

Closer to home, I have, since school days, been a fan of Peugeot cars and have owned seven, over the years. I had decided to buy a new 504 station wagon, and it seemed apparent that I would get the best price for my sedan by selling it privately. The phone rang in response to my advertisement in the newspaper and I was barraged by an unending series of questions about the vehicle, what colour was it, did it have good tires, what was the state of the battery?... on and on it went for what seemed like thirty minutes, until I heard myself saying that I was, myself, something of a Peugeot enthusiast and if the gentleman didn't live too far away, it would be well worth his while to come and inspect it for himself... He asked: "Has the vehicle ever been in an accident?" "Of course not," I expostulated. The voice droned on: "What about the time you left the hand brake off and it rolled into a tree on your property up at Woodend?" Roger 'B...' Heagney! I might well have guessed, but I didn't, did I? I had no idea Roger had such an all encompassing knowledge of cars, and I still don't; bless his little cotton socks.

As I attended a Leonhardt concert in Austria, he recognised me and observed that I was a "long way from home." "Indeed so, sir," I said, "And perhaps you might care to join me to have a coffee after the concert?" He was whimsical: "Yes, or something stronger." It proved an entertaining diversion, so much so that I confided to him that in Australia he was affectionately known as "Uncle Gus." "Uncle Gus?" he repeated questioningly. "No, no, sorry," I said, "Not Uncle Gus rather Ooncle Goose!" to which he responded with a palpable undercurrent of malice: "Ooncle Goose?" Feeling I wasn't getting anywhere, I said, with commendable finality: "Yes, you know, Auntie Wanda – Ooncle Goose!" "Ah," he said. The moment passed, but it seemed then, as it still does, that the conversation was in dire need of rapid directional change.

So saying, let's skip to San Francisco: Roger and I were staying with the late Laurette Goldberg, (a long time friend of Uncle Gus, by the way), and she insisted we enjoy a meal at the famous Fisherman's Wharf, (sad to say that the area has been gutted by fire since our visit, though now rebuilt). Well, the meal was finished and I stood up to put on my overcoat and backed my large posterior fair into the elbow of a chap who was making a reasonably good attempt at feeding himself a spoonful of soup. Feeling the bump I turned to see an entire shirt front covered with soup! I lapsed into remarkable 'strine' and said, hastily: "I'm terribly sorry, mate, it's terrible having a big bum, isn't it?" "Uh?" he said, and Laurette came to my rescue: "Oh, I'd like you to meet my Australian friends; in Australia a bum means a derriere." "Why that's wonderful," he boomed, and rose with his hand outstretched in friendship. I should not have survived!

One could continue, ad nauseam, with long-winded anecdotal stories but one should at least attempt to show some restraint. Therefore, this story of my father's, at the now defunct Officer Cadet School, Balcombe, Victoria, will be reason to call a halt: "What's a Gnostic, Mac?" asked the Officer Commanding. Said my father:

"Sir, a Gnostic is a person who believes they have had a divine revelation from God, a person who believes that they are one of God's messengers on Earth." My father, as one of the Chaplains on the Base, had lectured the trainees for non-attendance at Church Parade and had issued an order that everyone would attend all future Church Parades. Unbeknownst to my father, deep exception to this order was taken by the Regimental Sergeant Major, who complained to the OC seeking personal exemption. My father was in the OC's office when the poor unsuspecting fellow was marched in by the adjutant. Said the OC: "Stand easy RSM." "Sir," the instant response. The OC continued: "RSM, have you had a divine revelation from God; do you believe you are one of God's chosen messengers on Earth?" The RSM snapped to attention: "No Sir." "Very good RSM, attend Church Parade! Dismissed." The RSM stiffened, threw the automatic salute, and marched out, with only an inconsequential twitching of his mighty moustache suggesting demonstrative disagreement.

INSTRUMENT AGEING

*"Old wood best to burn, old wine to drink, old friends
to trust, and old authors to read." – attributed to
Alonso of Arago by Sir Francis Bacon,
Apothegms, 97 [1624]*

As of the twenty-first century the scientific fraternity may agree that
everything in our world, and in the universe as we comprehend it,
indeed, expectantly, the entire universe itself, will eventually age and
die. Radioactive substances may have a half-life of so many thousand
years but they, too, will eventually lose their radioactivity and become
inert. So why should we, as intelligent and educated human beings,
pretend that the violin family of stringed instruments, rather than
undergoing a gradual breakdown over time, are supposed to improve
with age?

It is important to state that this can not be so; indeed, if it were, it
would equate in importance to the creation of the fabled, but fanciful,
perpetual motion machine! To direct the musicians' attitude to the
untruthfulness of this concept, however, seems not so easy, for an
essential requirement is to close from the mind as many irrelevant
influences as possible, such as, for example, the admiration that we
all have for olden day stringed instrument makers of the standing of
Stradivari, Guarneri, Amati, and many others. No one is condemning
their achievement, indeed, they doubtless should be lauded as great
makers. But it must be remembered that they were the children
of a different age, the Baroque, and that they never could have
anticipated their instruments functioning under the conditions and
expectations we demand of them today. In fact, if it were possible
to 'time warp' these old makers to the present, to hear how one of
their instruments sounds now, in the hands of say a Nigel Kennedy,
or Yo-Yo Ma, they would not recognise the sounds as of their own
conception or making. Instinctively and logically we know that this
must be so because of the number of differences in the way the

instruments have been changed and 'set up' and also, importantly, because of a general elevation in pitch over the intervening time frame. A widespread rise in pitch, in Europe, as occurred at the end of the seventeenth century, necessitated dramatic design changes, as exhibited by the work of both stringed and keyboard makers, and thereafter arose a more standardised approach to both instrument making and appropriate pitch, nowhere near as standardised as we are able to achieve in the twenty-first century, however, and it required an industrial revolution to create and cater to a true concept of standardisation.

Any interested student might readily establish the various changes to the string family set-up, by consulting The New Grove Dictionary of Music and Musicians. Therein it may be established that, a violin by Stradivari, modified to perform in the twenty-first century will comprise the following original items only as having been crafted by the master: the back, the belly, the sides (ribs), and the scroll.

The changes surely speak for themselves: The neck (even the method of attaching it to the body) discarded! New pegs, new nut, larger fingerboard, sound post (larger diameter), bass bar (larger dimension), bridge (radically different in design), tail piece, tail gut (nylon), end pin, plus four modern steel strings and tuning adjusters. The concept of the stringing alone, takes the whole sound experience to a different dimension – for without strings there is obviously no sound! Not only are the strings now made of metal, making possible a longer speaking length but they speak as much as a whole tone higher in pitch than was required of their baroque originals. Where is the logic in that? Pythagoras, in the sixth century BC demonstrated that, for every octave increase in pitch, string speaking lengths would halve for wires of the same diameter, mass, and tension; not get longer! To top it off these new strings are being played with a different shaped, increased tensioned, and heavier bow, and one, moreover, furnished with about a third more horse hair than its namesake from the Baroque.

With these modernised instruments then, we are hearing an amalgam, or a hybrid: something of the work of the original maker, the modifier, the development of new technology, the inherent skill of the performer, and, if on record, the whimsy of the recording technician, to modify and adjust the recorded sound, and how aged or up to date his equipment is, so to do.

Thus, it may be postulated that the original Stradivari sound has been permanently lost to us! Yet we still continue to be drawn, inexplicably, to a fawning appreciation of his opus, to the extent that there is a prevailing perception that the 'art of making' is now lost. Any loss is certainly not due to the age of his instruments, as may be understood.

Stringed instruments are made of wood, (apart from their strings, of course!). Wood has many interesting properties some of which we might care to consider.

ELASTIC MEMORY

This sounds like modern 'techno' speak, however, the Ancients were very well aware of the phenomenon. Some woods have better memories than others. Yew, for example, from which the English made their longbows, was utilised because, having been pulled taught by the archer, it tried to regain its position of rest with great rapidity and thus shoot an arrow a far distance. The English long bowmen were feared archers but they were rendered less effectual in the Crusades because the Yew wood lost its elastic memory in the hot, dry climate of the Middle East, and the bowmen consequently lost their firepower. Interestingly, the Yew bows regained their lost memory on the bowmen returning home to England's colder climate. A violin bow, most often made from Brazilian Pernambuco, also demonstrates this elastic memory, the arch of the wood increasing on loosening the hair. The North American Indians used Osage orange (bois d'arc) for their hunting bows and this wood, too, demonstrates excellent elastic memory; it may also, I suggest, make excellent violin bows. Though not as dense and fine grained as players might prefer, it would, nevertheless, respond very efficiently as a bow. Various Australian desert species of *Acacia* have been used to make excellent violin family bows. It must be observed that European Spruce is not noted for its elastic memory but it is just this very characteristic that is sought from it when it performs as a violin belly. The belly has to be carefully shaped and graded in order to coax it to more effectively perform its function, and therein lies the art of the luthier.

Drawing an analogy with a loud speaker, (more obviously a bass speaker) one can see the centre of the cone moving in and out in response to electronic driving, the whole being mounted on excellently elastic, rubberised, speaker outer edges, and hence we see great efficiency of movement! This pumping action is exactly what is required of the belly or soundboard of a stringed instrument.

HYGROSCOPIC INSTABILITY

More techno speak meaning, the wood, if exposed to moisture, absorbs some but not all of what is on offer. Again, the Ancients were well aware of this property of wood. When dried, the wood gives back the moisture it has gained, and maybe more, so that it can become very brittle. It is possible to slow down the rate of absorption and expulsion of moisture by the wood, but impossible to inhibit it completely. Enter the 'finish' used on the timber, which if cleverly conceived, serves both as a retardant to the speed of change in moisture content, and a protective film which not only stops the wood from becoming dirty from being constantly handled by human hands, but cleverly enhances its appearance into the bargain. When evaluating a soft wood such as European Spruce, cut on the quarter, it is important to consider the number of grain lines to the inch, for this has a bearing on moisture absorption rates, the pithy material between winter growth lines being much more like a sponge! Every string player in love with his or her instrument has observed that their cherished baby behaves differently in different environments, (aside from different acoustic environments), when playing at home, from one day to the next, and between summer and winter. Frustrating though this may be, there is naught to be done to rectify the situation other than provide an unchanging atmosphere. It may give the impression that the wood is alive and always on the move, but it is, in fact, dead, and always on the move. Of course, we remember the ancient Egyptians used manipulation of the moisture content of the wood to split their rocks. This aspect of the behavioural properties of wood was, and remains, a potent force indeed!

Cross Grain Stiffness

Everyone has observed the divers on the swimming pool diving board and how trusting they are that the board won't snap. The grain of the wood runs along the length of the board – if it ran crosswise, the board would snap like a carrot. It is this characteristic that the instrument maker has to always bear in mind in his choice of timber, the drying process of the timber, the design geometry of the instrument to both produce the required sound and to hold at bay this particular shortcoming of his chosen material. The application of a suitable finish has only a slight effect regarding improvement to cross grain stiffness, for splits and cracks will appear in the belly (and back, too, particularly with larger instruments) at some time in the future. This can happen either through accident or careless handling, and clearly through shrinkage of timber over time. It is readily observed that the cracks always run along the grain lines, never across, but it is the lack of strength across the grain that causes the cracks along the grain. The only possible manner of rectifying this situation is to laminate the belly material. Unfortunately, this has significant implications on the tone we seek, such that the instrument would have to be completely redesigned because the speed of sound travels twice as fast along the grain as across, and this is partly the reason why violin family instruments are still being made the shape that they are.

Clearly, with wood, we are dealing with a far from perfect material from the aspect of being 'built to last,' yet coming to terms with these limitations is part of the challenge facing makers, and to a surprisingly large extent, players also, for it is they who are entrusted with the intelligent husbandry of an instrument. Ultraviolet rays and oxygen are known to be major factors in the decaying process, affecting the make up of our instruments. This decaying process, properly called oxidation, eats away at steel leaving behind the red dust we call rust, produces the white powder on lead called lead oxide, the green accretions on copper and brass called verdigris, and the ever darkening of timber grain till it becomes almost black, as if it had been scorched by a hot iron. Eventually everything returns to the earth (we are doubtless indulged by being allowed to keep gold and platinum!).

When instruments are newly finished or recently rebuilt, there is the well known phenomenon known variously as 'playing in,' blooming,' 'settling down,' 'developing,' and so on. We can delude ourselves that this continues for ever, but sadly this is just not the case, the developing too settles down and reaches a plateau, which it may or may not sustain for a substantial period of time. Inevitably frustration over some aspect of imperfection will creep in and finally, the instrument is taken off to the 'master craftsperson' who miraculously appears to breathe in new life for another term, which is, of course, yet further proof of the reality we are considering.

I believe it is a truism that performers who restrict themselves to playing old instruments are playing those instruments out, whilst those who play new instruments are playing them in. If new instruments are well thought out and constructed they will readily play in, be in good condition for a considerable plateau period of time, and then start their downhill run, hopefully to a worthy retirement. (No photographs of the museum piece are permitted, of course, because of the damaging effects of ultraviolet radiation).

Two other major factors continue to cloud our thinking on the matter. Dealers, who are not makers, but who are in the second-hand selling game, have played an important role in pushing values of desirable old instruments through the roof, almost out of reach for even the rich to consider; and Nostalgia, our own developed sense about things old and beautiful which we are constantly being told can never be created again to the same level of excellence. But this is only a half-truth! We are certainly not running short of capable craftsmen, but, on the other hand, we are ever more rapidly exhausting the natural resources of suitable timber!

Of course, there is yet more to consider... Professor Richard Dawkins, Oxford luminary and proud atheist, has said that:

> We are all atheists about many gods, it's just that I
> have gone one step further and eliminated all gods.

Would that we instrument makers could claim such a clear-sighted and practical clientele.

CATNAP TWO

The briefest siesta

Andrew Bernard, self styled as 'The Student,' and a contributor to this work, not least through his careful evaluation and emendation of the draft manuscript, has, for reasons known only to himself, determined to grant me the appellation of Master. It is a mantle that causes the fidgets of unworthiness. Nevertheless, his many communications have engaged me to respond, however inadequately, and, of course, his persona, knowledge, and friendship continue to hold my best regard. This spiel would mean little without an exemplar:

IN THE FULLNESS OF THE DAY

The student approached the Master with humility and not a little nervousness bearing a query relating to the manner of giving the instrument to speak, its voic'ing, so as to talk in a quaintly modern manner. 'O Master,' began the student, for the 'O' of the vocative case was still current at that time, and was indeed a requirement in correct circles: 'O Master, may one enquire as to the manner of voic'ing th'instrument, like unto how much, so to make it speak as though with the tongues of very angels: Izekiel, Manakeil, Gabriel, Ashtoth, and Jurazett?' The reader is here advised that not one of the fore mentioned celestial beings ever existed, but let that not detain him.

Occupied with refining a key balance to the very prick of perfection, the Master replied: 'I could'na gie a Rat's Arse, nae more,' with a good deal of more kindly intent than is rendered by the mere transcription of the utterance. At this, the Student was enlightened, bowed, and proceeded to miraculously voice the instrument near complete, it being set before him as a task, the doing of which had become odious to the Master as the Meerschaum pipe of repute appeared to have developed a defect, would not ignite, and may have to be replaced, which as the sensitive reader will know, is never the same.

Having gained enlightenment through the teaching of the Master, the Student completed his task to a degree of harmonious perfection otherwise heard only in the biblical efforts of M. Don'agle, latterly of the Americas. As desired, the instrument spake forth with power and rhetoric, and a smoothness of voicing throughout the compass, on manuals both high and low, that could only be compared to the silken flush of a virgin's breast, if one is able so to ascertain – and simultaneously forgive – the paucity of the metaphor.

Thereafter, the Student attempted some cleverly composed Preludes and Fugues by J. S. Bach, and, in the fullness, completed his darg, as a day of honest labour is known in this country. The Master then but simply indicated that it was time for them to go home and investigate further the methods of imprisonment used in the '60s, a favourite diversion of the Master in his precious spare time.[1] Taking the offer to indicate the faint

1 Andrew here makes reference to the 60s television series *The Prisoner*, with its well deserved cult following, and to the puissantly real probability of spotting a Thomas Goff harpsichord in a particular episode.

possibility of some very small degree of approval, the Student arose and they left together.

This is the way in which knowledge of the craft is handed down from master to disciple, and how the hard learn'd secrets are preserv'd for the eternal generations and the children of The Art.

Your tireless correspondent, etc.[2]

On my querying the 'O' in the above email, Andrew responded:

'O' is the correct vocative particle... Oh is the correctly rendered orthography for an exclamation in English. Example: 'Oh!' exclaimed the virgin upon encountering an object considerably larger than her girlish imagination had led her to consider previously.

---

2 Email received 22 January 2008.

A CASE FOR THE HARPSICHORD

Avoiding the inferiority complex

The year is 2003. Attending a harpsichord Master Class, I was bemused, even nonplussed, to hear the lecturer refer to the clavichord as "J. S. Bach's favourite instrument." This statement was just a little too crisp for me to swallow. Being that rare combination of brazen, but sensitive, harpsichord fanatic that I am, I found myself unable to sleep as a consequence of this outrageous claim and, instead, was drawn to the alchemy of the Apple Avenger, so that I might venture to compose a bold retort. I am aware that, even though were I to write eloquently about this anomaly, or some other musicological fallacy, any remonstrations of mine would hardly lead to a puncturing of the intelligentsia's indifference balloon; but my arrows points have now been honed and that being the case, I shall proceed and remain hopeful, if not optimistic.

The Early Music Movement, or Historically Informed Performance (HIP) as it is now more properly known, should doubtless expunge the above educator from their good graces for harbouring so subjective a thought. In the face of such a cavalier attitude, by a supposed supporter of HIP, we might reasonably question whether HIP has actually encapsulated anything of substance, and importantly, permanence, that may help crystallise the layman's sense of reality, for the journey into the future.

The aims and good intentions of HIP are not in dispute here, and much of real value does seem to have become established in current early music performance practice. Indeed, at one level, a student musician may expect to be sternly censured if the proclaimed 'rules' pertaining to this or that music are not known or not adhered to. Nevertheless, and from a similar perspective, those who, unthinkingly, and freely, continue to juxtapose the keyboard instruments used for playing J. S. Bach, when the choice should logically reflect the musical practice of the Master, seem somehow, to escape criticism!

The choice of instrument appears to have eluded precise clarification by earlier writers, and players are still not expected to embrace the matter as a vital 'musical fulcrum' in staging their performances. Are we really saying that 'the essence of the man and the tools he used are of no account,' and all that matters is the music he has bequeathed us? Perhaps not, for even a first year student of music would instantly reject any suggestion that Beethoven was a banjo player, and thank God for that! But then, Paganini was a guitarist, was he not?

Are there mitigating circumstances we can pretend excuse our lecturer's commission? Being post 11 September, 2001, we have, willy-nilly, become part of an ever changing New World Order that inclines us to be apathetic about seeking an understanding of noted personalities of the past, let alone the present, and seemingly, any such consolidated concepts are summarily tossed out like the baby with its bath water. Now we are being bombed by terrorists for our lack of understanding. We appear to be so inundated with endless possibilities for 'something or other' that our cognisance of the fundamentals seems to have been dissipated by an 'anything goes' attitude; especially when elements of our society make us feel like mere numbers (and odd numbers, at that). We become strangely disturbed when we read that a computer, (meaningfully called Deep Blue), has now defeated the Grand Master of world chess! Still, on a good day, we may fancy that, did we but possess the genius, we too would welcome the conditions in which Haydn found himself when working first for the Esterhazy's, as he recorded: "there were no other musicians around so I was forced to be original." (Unfortunately, in our state of dozy awareness, we discern the cautionary whisper: "Such a position is not for you, you old jackdaw," and so yet another fantasy slips from our grasp).

It is commonplace to imagine that logical thinking invariably proves to be the undoing of intuition, though let us not confuse intuition with originality! But then, the statement, 'Bach's favourite instrument was the clavichord' should not be taken as an original thought of our lecturer; it had been made by many others, time and time again. So, I would suggest we ask the question: Should we allow intuition to play a part in our deliberations? I believe the response has to be in the affirmative, however, our intuition should be tempered by what facts we know, rather than by idle speculation. The claim that, had he known it, Bach would have written for the modern piano and preferred to listen to that instrument over and above the instruments with which he was actually familiar, is among the grossest of 'logical' distortions. Deviously, it purports to be intuitive, so as to appeal to those who visualise and lean on the logic as being real. Supporting the logic are statements such as; the piano is touch responsive and able to be played with infinite dynamic graduation, from *ppp* to *FFF*; it has far greater sustain than either the harpsichord or clavichord, and is provided with a sostenuto pedal to prove it; it stays in tune better and it is undeniably more reliable than its archaic cousin, one can execute a genuine legato, and so on. It has even been extrapolated that if J. S. Bach had been composing in 1850 we could be confident that he would have left us a wealth of 'original' piano music, beautifully written for that instrument. I would suggest to these advocates, however, that they would not necessarily recognise the authorship of such music as from the pen of J. S. Bach. Both the instrument, and fashion of the times, would have required from him a new and different compositional approach!

Writing in the catalogue of his keyboard instrument collection of 1892, Morris Steinert declares:

> It can be maintained with apodictic certainty that Bach was always accustomed to claim the highest pretensions in regard to the capacity of all instruments used by him, and that he had without doubt weighty artistic reasons for preferring in such a distinguished way the clavichord for the execution of clavier compositions.

There is no doubt that this catalogue is an important historical document, and I am privileged to own an original volume, but the above passage is an excellent example of the fact that, 'one simply should not believe, at face value, all that one hears or reads.' Many writers, (some of whom we might well have expected to know better, for example, Zuckermann, *The Modern Harpsichord*), have been guilty of referring to the clavichord as, "a favourite instrument of J. S. Bach" (Zuckermann, 19). More recently, Anthony Baines (Baines, 71) says:

> It (the clavichord) is today again readily obtainable for all who like a small, quiet, and authentic instrument for playing, for example, the keyboard music of J. S. Bach, who is said to have preferred the clavichord to any other keyboard instrument apart from the organ.

Baines further claims that Bach wrote his '48' for the clavichord. (Baines, 73). Although not credited as such, the reference by Baines to Bach's preference, appears very possibly to be a grab from the biographical essay on J. S. Bach, published in 1802 by Johann Nicolas Forkel [1749–1818]. Forkel, could not have known this from first hand knowledge however, for he was just one year old when Bach died. The New Grove notes that much of the material Forkel used in writing about J. S. Bach, he obtained from two of Bach's sons, Carl Philipp Emanuel and Wilhelm Friedemann. Unenlightened thinkers seem to gravitate toward such statements of dubious integrity and repeat the falsities, like gossip, without giving thought as to their accuracy or reliability of sources, if indeed, any at all are offered or acknowledged, and in the process, overlooking potential damage to later generations. Again, Oscar Thompson in his *Cyclopedia* declares:

It [the clavichord] was a favourite of J. S. Bach and
Mozart.

Now that Mozart also makes the list as a devotee, with whom
will it stop, I wonder?

A plethora of writers seem to have simply confused their Bachs!
Perhaps they incorrectly attribute Dr Charles Burney's writings
as referring to J. S. Bach, when, in *The Present State of Music in
Germany, The Netherlands and The United Provinces*, 1773, he records
his visit to C. P. E. Bach:

> After dinner, which was elegantly served and
> cheerfully eaten, we repaired once more to the
> music room where I prevailed upon him to sit
> down at his Silbermann clavichord, and *favourite
> instrument*, and he played, with little intermission,
> 'til near 11 o'clock at night. During the performance
> he became so possessed his eyes fixed, his under
> lip fell and drops of effervescence distilled from his
> countenance. [The italics are mine.]

Burney was quite right! The clavichord was C. P. E. Bach's
favourite instrument, but this was a very different clavichord from
that which was in common use in his father's lifetime. In addition,
it should not need stating that C. P. E. Bach's musical aesthetic also,
was very different from that of his father. The early clavichord was
a small, single strung, double or triple 'fretted' instrument of four
octave compass. (Double and triple fretting refers to the fact that in
such instruments, two or three adjacent keys are provided with only
one string, or pair of unison strings, between them). It was only in
the 1720s, and more particularly the second half of the eighteenth
century, that German and the Scandinavian builders 'took on' the
development of the instrument and eventually produced a full
five octave sized instrument with 2×8' courses of strings to each

note. Some makers even went so far as to include an additional 1×4′ string course in the bottom octave or so, which was intended to add definition and to brighten the bass. Interestingly, C. P. E. Bach, recorded his dislike of these 4′ strings (Boalch, also *The New Grove*). The inventory compiled at the time of J. S. Bach's death, lists no such developed clavichord, or indeed, a clavichord of any size whatsoever, as being among his possessions, though it does record he owned no less than eight harpsichords!

It may be recalled by some readers that old encyclopaedias, (for example *Chambers Encyclopaedia*, often confuse J. S. Bach's *Das Wohltemperierte Clavier* as being written for the clavichord. Anthony Baines repeats it! (see above). The English translation of the German word klavier or clavier is keyboard! (My German born colleague, Jürgen Trinkkeller, advises that the eighteenth century spelling of the word Klavier with either a K or a C is of no significance whatsoever). Leaving the common mistranslation aside, it is difficult to imagine the '48' being conceived for the type of clavichord available to J. S. Bach, when such an instrument did not have all the notes required by the compositions or even a full complement of strings for each note of its compass. Importantly, and devotees of the clavichord need not be offended, if a player strikes a key with more or less force, the pitch of the string being struck will noticeably alter, and whilst this offers the player the possibility of *bebung*, or vibrato, this very characteristic rules against the precise setting of a temperament implied by the concept of a 'well tempered' keyboard. One can not 'well temper' a violin for example, because, apart from the 'open' strings, the player 'makes' all the notes. What relevance, therefore, can there be to the term 'well tempered' in the title of Bach's WTC, to a collection of clavichord pieces, where both tuner and player make their notes? (though, admittedly, not to quite the same degree as on the violin). No! The early clavichord was essentially regarded as a practice instrument until well into the second half of the eighteenth century. I am not trying to say that the instrument did not (as it still does) have its own particular charm.

Its response to sensitivity of touch and *bebung* were appreciated by many, and there can be no doubt that instruments were treasured by their owners in those times, just as they are today. But, J. S. Bach's favourite instrument? There is insufficient evidence to confirm such a belief or asseveration!

There is, however, ample evidence, in J. S. Bach's own hand, to indicate that he was writing here for the harpsichord, here for the organ, but nowhere, specifically, for the clavichord. This is not to say that the music could not or should not be played on a clavichord, assuming it was provided by its maker with the requisite compass of keys. To be pedantic, there still exists an original clavichord with two manuals and pedals which could sound music which Bach specifically composed for the organ. Yet if such performances were attempted in public today one can only speculate as to the reaction of organ buffs, not to mention music critics! And here we meet part of the problem; the clavichord simply does not have the strength of voice to do justice to the breadth of the musical palette, that J. S. Bach sought for his organ music and, indeed, his harpsichord music also. Do I hear piano buffs accusing me of borrowing their old argument, to use in a criticism of the clavichord?

Of course, in the end, whether a performance works, or not, on this or that instrument, still remains a matter of personal taste, hence we should take every care to remove all perversity from our musical judgements and thereby, perchance, achieve 'good taste'! So, though the clavichord acquired an important repertoire, specifically its own, we should not forget that this did not occur until the second half of the eighteenth century and then it was seen as the keyboard instrument that best expressed the style galante from which strict polyphony was eliminated. (see *The New Grove*). The pianoforte/fortepiano was still to catch up!

Some commentators have seen the Prelude in C major, from Book One of Bach's *Das Wohltemperierte Clavier*, as the classic piece of clavichord writing and, indeed, there is no doubt that it can sound very engaging when played well on that instrument. There is opportunity to demonstrate one's cantabile in the best J. S. Bach manner and, too, one can employ the instrument's bebung to telling musical effect. On the other hand, I would suggest that it may also be seen as a classic piece of harpsichord writing through which Bach was desirous of informing his listeners, and students, of the 'gravitas' of his concept of a good harpsichord and, to drive home right from the outset (the very first piece in the volume), the seriousness with which he regarded the composition of his 'well tempered' preludes and fugues. Over time, the collection expanded from twenty four to forty eight preludes and fugues, altogether an acknowledged spectacular achievement of J. S. Bach that has been described as 'The Bible' of Western Music. This C Major Prelude clearly exploits the gradual increase in sonority, common to all good harpsichords, as it moves to its resolution in the bass. This increase in bass sonority is not present in the clavichord because the design parameters of its 'musical geometry' simply deny it the possibility. These parameters include a much smaller soundboard area, shorter strings, and most particularly, the point of attack of the tangent serves to denote the speaking length of the string which creates a nodal point that, by its very nature, severely inhibits the fundamental response of a string at the notated pitch. This point of attack creating the speaking length also limits the amount of energy a player can impart to the acoustic system and this also limits the partials, or overtones, produced by the string. The result is a bass sonority that becomes ever weaker as the pitch of the notes played becomes lower, and hence, the gravitas of the piece may only be imagined. Acoustically, there is no solution to this shortcoming, and amplification does nothing to help!

This C Major Prelude is also an example of a composition in *style brisé* (that is, in the style of the plucked lute) so it seems odd to obfuscate the obvious by suggesting this style should be attempted on a struck clavichord (or piano) when there is an all plucking harpsichord standing by, unresisting and within easy reach, waiting patiently for its keys to be touched.

To digress for a moment; it has always struck me as odd that, since the advent of the 'modern' harpsichord, in 1889, some famous and some not so famous people have actively voiced their disenchantment with the instrument, variously describing it as: "that cage for flies," "two skeletons copulating on a tin roof," "striking a fork on a toast rack," or "as subtle as a Mack truck," and so on. Maybe contemporary detractors are suffering from what might be described as jackhammer jarred senses? Still, I console myself that they have surely been outnumbered, and of course, there is always the good harpsichord sound competing with the inevitable not so good. Surely there can be no disgrace about admiring the sound of the harpsichord; in historical terms, those who do so keep good company, for it took nearly one hundred years and a major shift in musical style for the pianoforte to finally win the stage to itself. (Many thanks, Ludwig!) I remember in the 1990s, taking a harpsichord on tour through China, with Roger Heagney, and how readily the populace appeared to accept the sound of the instrument. The plucked string seemed more immediately agreeable to non-western ears; it is the hammered piano that is alien to Eastern musical culture. For recent generation Westerners, the reverse is true. Our ears have had to become accustomed to the plucked sounds of the harpsichord and to politely ignore the outbursts of bigoted piano lovers. Meanwhile, many modern builders continue striving to smooth out the harpsichord's tonal palette to make it less raucous and more musical: "More fundamental and less fizz, if you please!" And they still get frustrated, when there is no possibility of achieving that elusive, though supposedly appropriate, feminine cadence.

But to continue, it seems that from quite early on in his career, J. S. Bach actually championed the harpsichord and took it upon himself to educate the common man, the man in the street, about its possibilities. It should be clearly stated that the music he composed for it, seals the harpsichord's place as his equal first love with the organ. Consider the following:

Φ He wrote more toccatas for keyboard alone than for keyboard and pedal.

Φ In the flute sonatas he challenged the convention of simply providing a figured bass and decided to fully "write out" the harpsichord part in the later sonatas, thereby effectively creating a trio sonata.

Φ In the violin sonatas he went a step further and gave one whole movement to the harpsichord alone, a display of favouritism not accorded the violin.

Φ He crowned the harpsichord alone with a transcendent cadenza in the 5th *Brandenburg Concerto*. (A concerto, nominally purporting to be shared equally, by each of harpsichord, flute and violin).

Φ Let us not forget the coffee shop performances for solo and multiple claviers; yet another first! Concerti for three and four harpsichords? The concept seems outrageous, but what a wonderfully creative advertising gimmick, one almost guaranteed to attract an audience to the performances!

Φ The genius of thought and emotion he invested in the music of the *Partita in B Minor*, the *Italian Concerto* and the *Goldberg Variations*, for example. (In these works Bach expressly called for a two manual harpsichord).

Φ We should surely not overlook the sixteen transcriptions for solo harpsichord, after concerti by various composers, for each one is a masterly transformation of its original, and worthy of a secure place in a modern harpsichord player's repertoire. There are but six similar conceptual transcriptions for the organ!

Φ *Die Kunst der Fuge* – Gustav Leonhardt's elegant solution in claiming that the entire work was written for the harpsichord, as a matter of course, and where the writing demanded, a second harpsichord was called for in the score, dispels any ambiguity and effectively denudes the slightly 'dotty' string quartet scenario. So we have here yet another monumental achievement with the composer presenting the harpsichord in full bloom!

From consideration of these points alone then, why should we doubt that J. S. Bach held the harpsichord in the highest esteem, indeed loved the instrument, demonstrated its potential and elevated its status to that of a concerto instrument? Strange, is it not, to consider that anyone alive today, and professing musical sensibilities, should yet place themselves out of step with the greatest musician the world has ever known, by actually declaring a dislike of the harpsichord? Yes, I know there are those who champion Mozart or Beethoven as the greatest composer, but I think otherwise, and I am not alone. I warmed to the comment of Lewis Thomas, MD, who wrote, in relation to what we might send to others in space as representative of mankind's intelligence, that he would send Bach's music:

> ... all of Bach, streamed out into space, over and
> over again. We would be bragging, of course, but
> it is surely excusable for us to put the best possible
> face on at the beginning of such an acquaintance.

I should add that I have listened carefully and with open interest to performances of the '48' on organ, clavichord and piano, and although acceptable from an academic point of view, (Clavier simply meaning keyboard) never once have I been convinced, when they were not played on a harpsichord, that I was listening to anything other than a transcription, literal or otherwise. In this connection, it is interesting to note that a preference for performance on German style harpsichords is now gaining acceptance and the increasing availability of excellent sounding reproductions of such instruments will be heard to present this case better than any further amount of verbiage. There is still much to be done in this area of instrument building and the instruments of the Hass family, and Christian Zell, both from Hamburg, and Johann Heinrich Harrass from Grossbreitenbach, loom large as examples of the kind of harpsichord J. S. Bach would have played on and gained his inspiration from, and been moved by. In recent times the discerning harpsichord 'buff' certainly no longer yearns to hear J. S. Bach's music played on yet another late eighteenth century French sounding harpsichord!

Readers might care to refer to the book *Landowska on Music* for its author's intuitive comments on the choice of instrument for the performance of the music of J. S. Bach – they are nothing if not passionate.

So, notwithstanding my bias as a harpsichord maker towards this issue, I believe I have presented a scenario that is, at the least, easier to accept as a plausible reality, rather than to claim otherwise!

Nota bene. Performers aplenty still persist in looting Bach's harpsichord works as appropriate for the piano repertoire, presenting them in both concerts and recordings with gay abandon and without apology. What is more, their performances are then promulgated to an unsuspecting public by courtesy of national radio broadcasters. I believe both protagonists are guilty of either gross musical ignorance, or bad taste, or perhaps both! Gustav Leonhardt once described the practice of playing harpsichord music on the piano as: "amoral."

Bach, being dead, cannot respond! This obvious statement is not intended to trivialise the subject in the slightest, but rather to make the point that we all take shelter behind the immutable fact of his silence. Where would we stand if he could return to speak his mind? Even a brief visit would confirm that the best stratagem to avoid the likely ignominy of cane or curse, would be to boldly emulate his practices, as we should know them, in all humility and without argument!

As Landowska bantered to Pablo Casals: "Well my dear, you continue to play Bach your way and I'll continue to play him his way!" (New York Times music critic, Harold Schonberg, was incorrect in his book, *The Great Pianists*, to record the exchange as being by Landowska to a 'female' Bach specialist. It has been suggested that he perhaps was thinking of Rosalyn Tureck?)

Postscriptum

It is now 2005 and the Canadian pianist, Angela Hewitt, has been on tour with the Australian Chamber Orchestra. Her program consisted of two Concerti for Piano [sic] and the Brandenburg Concerto No. 5, for Flute, Violin, and Piano [sic], by J. S. Bach. Curiously, the performance of the latter work also included a part for a continuo harpsichord!

I chanced upon an interview Ms Hewitt gave to ABC FM radio presenter, Damien Beaumont, who asked her if the question of playing Bach on the piano or the harpsichord was now settled once and for all. She replied that, yes, she thought so. She said she felt "sure that Bach would have been delighted to have today's excellent keyboards at his disposal." Damien Beaumont agreed. He then commented that whenever he tried to play the harpsichord he found himself searching, instinctively, for the sustaining pedal, to which Ms Hewitt responded that a sustaining pedal wasn't necessary when playing a harpsichord because the instruments were not supplied with dampers and that, therefore, any sustain, or lack thereof, was built-in! Damien Beaumont agreed! Ms Hewitt went on to say that she, however, played Bach in an historically informed manner, with due cognizance and understanding for ornaments, phrasing, and articulation. Damien Beaumont agreed.

After the interview concluded, Damien Beaumont declared just what a lovely person Angela Hewitt was, and how could anyone disagree with that observation? I might suggest that Damien Beaumont, also, is an equally lovely person. For the rest, I wonder whether such intellectual distortions should be allowed to continue unchecked, for it was similar misrepresentations of reality, coupled with a seemingly unshakeable belief that there existed a phenomenon best described as 'progress in art,' (and by extension, the tools at the artist's disposal), that created the myth of the validity of playing Bach on the piano in the first place.

I would hope that any sensitive harpsichordist or scholar will view with great discomfort the Angela Hewitt DVD *Bach on the Piano*, available as of 2008.

PLEYEL ET CIE

Une Grande Marque

A short note on the piano making firm of Pleyel and its people may be of interest. The original Pleyel company had been remarkable for having always been directed by musicians. It was founded in 1807 by the Austrian pianist and composer Ignace Pleyel [1757–1831] who, in 1821, formed a partnership with his son, Camille, [1788–1855]. The German pianist and composer Friedrich Kalkbrenner [1785–1849] joined the partnership in 1824. Camille Pleyel was succeeded in the control of the business by the pianist Auguste Wolff [1821–1887] who passed the directorship to his son-in-law, Gustave Lyon [1857–1936]. During the establishment of the business much valuable technical aid was given by the distinguished German born piano maker, Jean Henri Pape, this affiliation continuing until 1815, at which time Pape set up business on his own account, also in Paris.

The first half of the nineteenth century was a period of unparalleled development for the pianoforte. Pianos of all different shapes and sizes were experimented with, and there was a multiplicity of action types. By 1834 Pleyel claimed to employ 250 workers who produced a total of 1,000 pianos per year. That other great French maker, Sebastian Érard, had patented his double escapement or double repetition action in 1821 and this was eventually going to win the day over the simpler English grand action and the so called Viennese or Stein action. As one might expect, the house of Pleyel developed their own (a version of the English) action which was conceptually also a double repetition action, in that the hammer could be flung against the string a second time or indeed, however many times required, without the key having to return fully to its rest position, which was Érard's essential achievement. This action, with minor modifications, continued to be used by Pleyel into the twentieth century.

Chopin visited Paris in 1831 when he made his debut in Pleyel's concert hall, known as the Salle Pleyel. (This concert hall has, as of 2007, been restored by the French government, to mark the 200th year since the founding of the firm). Chopin professed himself enamoured of the touch and tonal qualities of the Pleyel grand and his influence engendered a tradition in the easy touch and peculiar singing tone of their instruments. Chopin owned a Pleyel concert grand dated 1839, which still survives. Auguste Wolff was later to improve the power of the Pleyel grands making them adequate to the requirements of the modern concert hall, without loss of those characteristic refined qualities.

Gustave Lyon continued the firm's tradition of ongoing research and development, producing a number of inventions specifically for the pianoforte. He also made other instruments including Kettle Drums and, importantly, Chromatic Harps. Another altogether outstanding Lyon creation was the Double Grand, effectively two grand pianos in one case, rectangular of form with a keyboard at either end, but with only one lid; such an instrument offers obvious advantages for duo piano works and as a teaching medium par excellence. Along with other big name piano houses Pleyel also made what are loosely known today as Art Pianos. With these instruments the greatest care was lavished on style and casework, with elaborate turnings, the finest filigree fret work, the use of marble and ceramics, tortoiseshell, and so on.

It is, perhaps, not generally recognised today that between 1820 and 1870 the French piano industry dominated the world's production of pianofortes both in relation to the quality of instruments and to the number of instruments made. Eventually, however, the mass production techniques of the New World assumed pre-eminence and the centre of the industry moved, holus-bolus, to the United States of America.

The principal French firms of Pleyel, Érard, and Gaveau continued to soldier on, Pleyel, having already absorbed the Parisian maker, Antoine Bord, merging with Gaveau and Érard in 1961, and then, in

1976, a licensing agreement was signed with the German company Schimmel, and production was carried on at Brunswick, with the new conglomerate styling themselves 'Les Grande Marques.' Pride of place was accorded to the Schimmel concert grand which was given the name Pleyel, whilst Schimmel proudly displayed a Pleyel concert grand Art Piano in the company's museum. More recently a new Pleyel factory opened in France and at the time of writing one can still purchase a Pleyel piano purpose built in France, though the future will perhaps see yet other developments.

It is the writer's opinion that the instruments produced by Pleyel were, indeed, of a uniformly high standard of design and workmanship and these criteria coupled with the firm's discerning knowledge of, and consistent use of the finest quality materials available, resulted in instruments of a special musical distinction and nobility. In addition to the concert harpsichord to be discussed below, the writer owns two Pleyel pianos, a boudoir grand c. 1865, and an upright c. 1905 each of which, of themselves, attest to this claim. As of the twenty first century, the House of Pleyel now enjoys Heritage status and a new chronicle of the company has just appeared in French, (2009), which is obtainable from the Pleyel web site. To top it all off, the anniversary of Chopin's birth in 1810 saw reproductions of early Pleyel Grands by two different fortepiano makers, Paul McNulty and Chris Maene, completed in 2010.

The Paris Exposition Universelle of 1889 was chosen by Pleyel to launch their new harpsichord, Gustave Lyon being the prime mover in the 'reconstruction' and presentation of the instrument. This exposition, of course, was organised by the French Government to commemorate the centenary of the French Revolution, and apart from the three locally made harpsichords exhibited by Pleyel, Érard, and one Louis Tomasini, was to be remembered for the opening of one of the then seven wonders of the modern world, the 300 metre Eiffel Tower. The three harpsichords from the exhibition are preserved in the State Institute for Music History in Berlin. Not one of them could be described as a close historical copy but rather

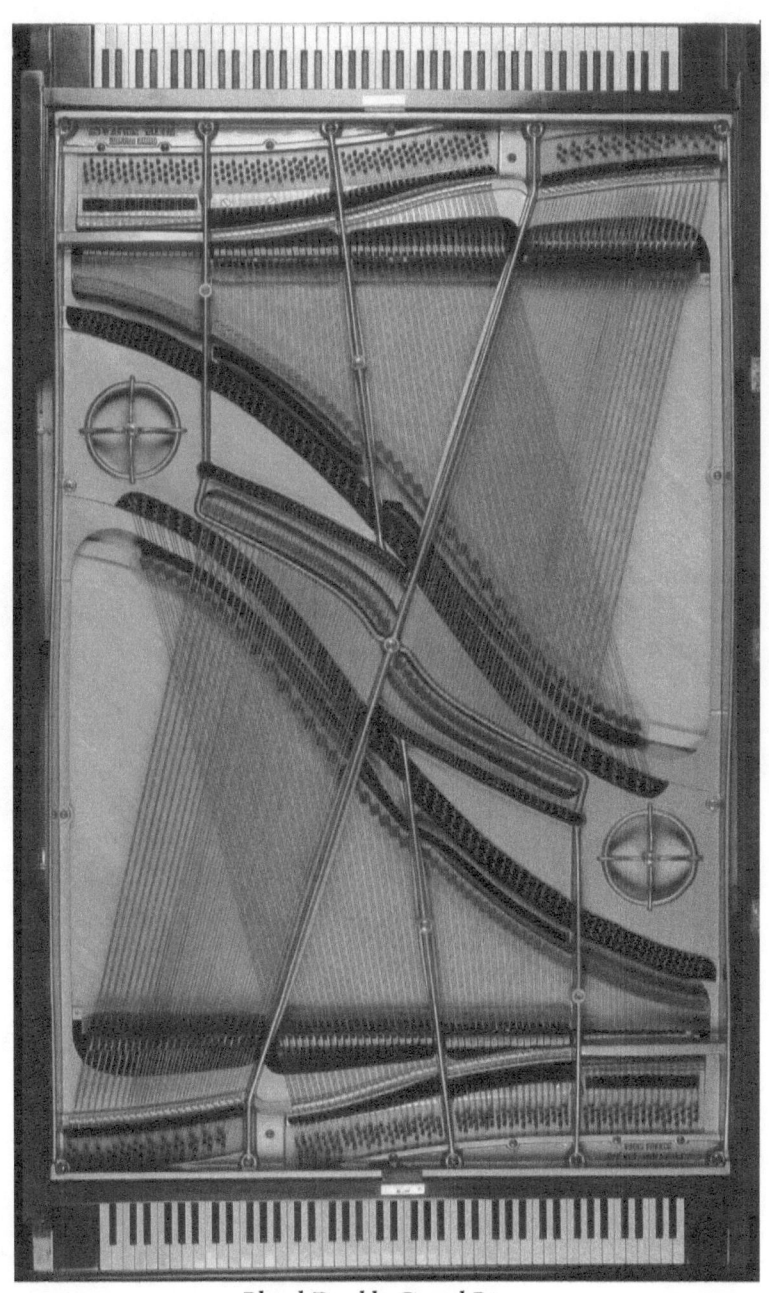

Pleyel Double Grand Piano

they represent the desires of their makers to demonstrate what a new look could do for the harpsichord. It was all part, perhaps, of a 'feeling in the air!'

Of these three, the Pleyel harpsichord stands apart as a totally sumptuous piece of work. The fully three-dimensional case sides, together with both sides of the lid, are all fabulously painted in the style of Watteau, whilst the instrument rests on an elaborately carved Louis XV stand, and sports an elegant lyre with six pedals. The keyboards have ivory naturals and ebony sharps. There are three sets of strings: 2×8' and 1×4' with an English style 'cut through' Lute Stop on the upper manual and a Harp or Buff Stop on the lower manual. The 8' strings are damped by a unique overhead damping system, which, incidentally, gives the lie to those who have claimed that the purpose of the overhead dampers was essential to more adequately control the greater amplitude of vibration of the strings of the 16' register. However, in these early design Pleyels, there is a version of overhead damper, but no 16' register! The c'' scaling of 333 mm, is 6 mm shorter than the 1769 Pascal Taskin, which was the instrument Pleyel used as the reference/starting point for their 'reconstruction.' In addition, a fully perfected fine-tuning system was incorporated for each of the 183 strings. I do not know how many such models were made by Pleyel, though it is difficult to imagine many more than a handful or two, so it is pleasing to record that one slightly later example, c. 1909, remains in private ownership in Australia!

Pleyel redesigned the six pedal model in the first quarter of the twentieth century producing a rather sad little creature which they called their 'Modèle Reduit.' I have seen one example at the Metropolitan Museum in New York, and I do not think I need to see another! The instrument of real interest, however, is the 'Landowska' model, and this was 'on the drawing board' as early as 1910.

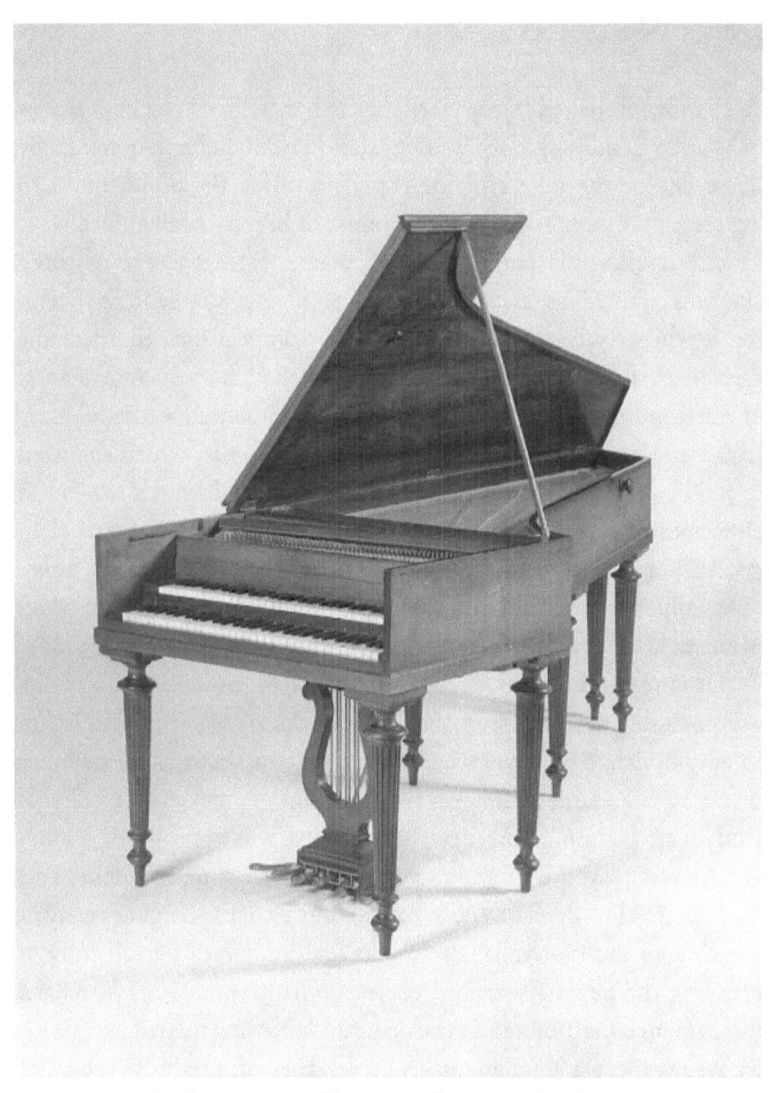

Pleyel et Cie Double Manual Harpsichord, 1891
Pleyel donated this instrument, in 1891, to the Royal Conservatory of
Music in Brussels (now the Musical Instruments Museum), where it
still resides. Note the stand of seven elegantly turned and reeded legs:
also note evidence of dysfunctional cheek disease.

To anyone interested in the world of the harpsichord the importance of Wanda Landowska [1879–1959] should need no further comment, however, for the sake of completeness and for the opportunity to express some personal comment, a note of brevity shall suffice!

Landowska was born in Poland where, from the age of three, she was trained as a pianist. At sixteen she was sent to Berlin for further study in counterpoint and composition. In 1900 she arrived in Paris and immediately established herself as a pianist of outstanding ability. She soon became acquainted with the early Érard and more especially, the Pleyel harpsichords, which she used in public performance for more than ten years. Although she found shortcomings in their musical resources they were, nevertheless, good enough to convince her of the truism that, in the main, music especially composed for the harpsichord sounded at its best when performed on that instrument.

Despite her diminutive stature of just 4 feet 10 inches, Landowska was not a shy person, besides which she had decided she had a mission to accomplish. She approached Gustave Lyon about the possibility of a larger and more sonorous instrument. After several years of study and planning, the new harpsichord was completed, and in 1912 it was played by Landowska, for the first time in public, at a Bach Festival in Breslau, (now Poland, but under German control at the time of the Festival). Landowska had immersed herself fully in bringing the new harpsichord project to fruition, visiting keyboard instrument collections and measuring and drawing instruments with M. Lamy, Pleyel's chief engineer. Pleyel, thereafter, always recorded her input in exquisite calligraphy on their instrument's jack rail. A translation reads:

> The lower register, called sixteen foot, was incorporated in the Pleyel harpsichords beginning

in 1912 at the request and according to the suggestions of Wanda Landowska.

There is no suggestion in this statement that Landowska claimed invention of the 16' stop, as some ignorant writers have suggested, only that she was eager that it be incorporated in her harpsichord.

Besides Polish, Landowska was fluent in German, English and French and whilst she retained an abiding love of her native country, she had become a true Francophile in that, as she said, she always thought and wrote in French. She also took French citizenship. Her compositions, however, reflect her Polish heritage and in 1951 she issued an LP entitled *Landowska Plays for Paderewski* which contains her homage to Polish music and musicians and she makes a point by playing Chopin's *Mazurka in C Major*, Op. 56 No. 2 on the harpsichord. It should here be observed that her performance was not an arrangement in any sense, indeed, there is a second Chopin Mazurka, the music of which does not exceed the five octave compass of the harpsichord nor the character of the piece require a sustaining pedal. Keyboard players could do worse than to make the discovery of these Mazurkas for themselves. They are wonderful Polish dances.

An intimate Viennese *Scherenschnitte* follows, depicting a young Landowska playing an early pre-1912 Concert Model Pleyel. One can easily imagine why Henri Lew – later to become her husband – became so captivated!

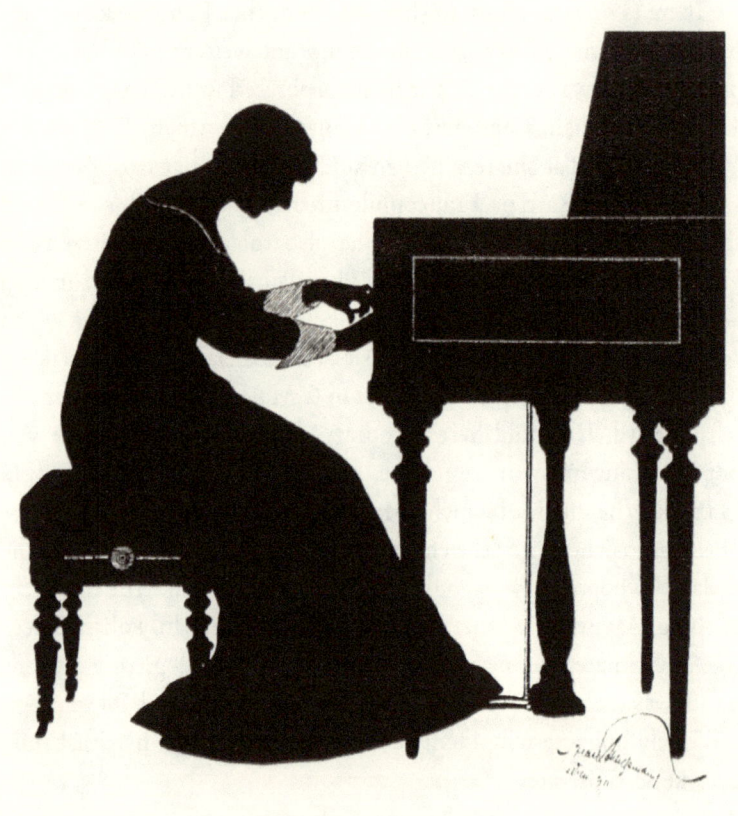

Wanda Landowska
Scherenschnitte by Hans Schliessmann, Vienna, 1911

Pleyel's 'Landowska' and 'Puyana' Models

I have coined the term 'Landowska Model' to differentiate the instruments made between 1912 and 1956 at which time a number of changes were made, particularly to the pedal specification, at the instigation of the Columbian harpsichordist Rafael Puyana. Puyana, Landowska's last student, requested an instrument from Pleyel in 1956 that incorporated positive action pedals. Instruments incorporating these changes made post 1956, we might happily describe as 'Puyana' models. He had the means to order two new instruments for himself. The harpsichord which I own is dated, in pencil on the lower keyboard, 14th August 1963, and so we shall look at it a little later.

Long before I acquired my Puyana Model I had in my possession an original 1937 Pleyel catalogue of the company's harpsichords, and this forms the basis of observations pertaining to the Landowska Model.

From my catalogue, the illustration shows the plan view of harpsichord No. 7. Fortunately, for this discussion, this is an early number. Unfortunately, there is no way of knowing precisely what year the number represents; it could well be the seventh Landowska Model or it may be the seventh harpsichord made in total, that is, there were six precursors, none with a 16' stop, which would make this a photograph of Landowska Model type number one. This particular picture must be quite well known by now, as apart from appearing in the American Diapason magazine it also graces *The New Grove Dictionary of Music and Musicians*. The American harpsichordist Alice Ehlers owned the tenth Landowska Model which is dated 1922; she and the harpsichord making their film debut in *Wuthering Heights*, in 1927.

The illustration of No. 7 shows the crease that may be seen in my catalogue, which I felt should be left untouched. The next illustration is of an instrument photographed one year after my catalogue date of 1937, which reveals some interesting changes. The

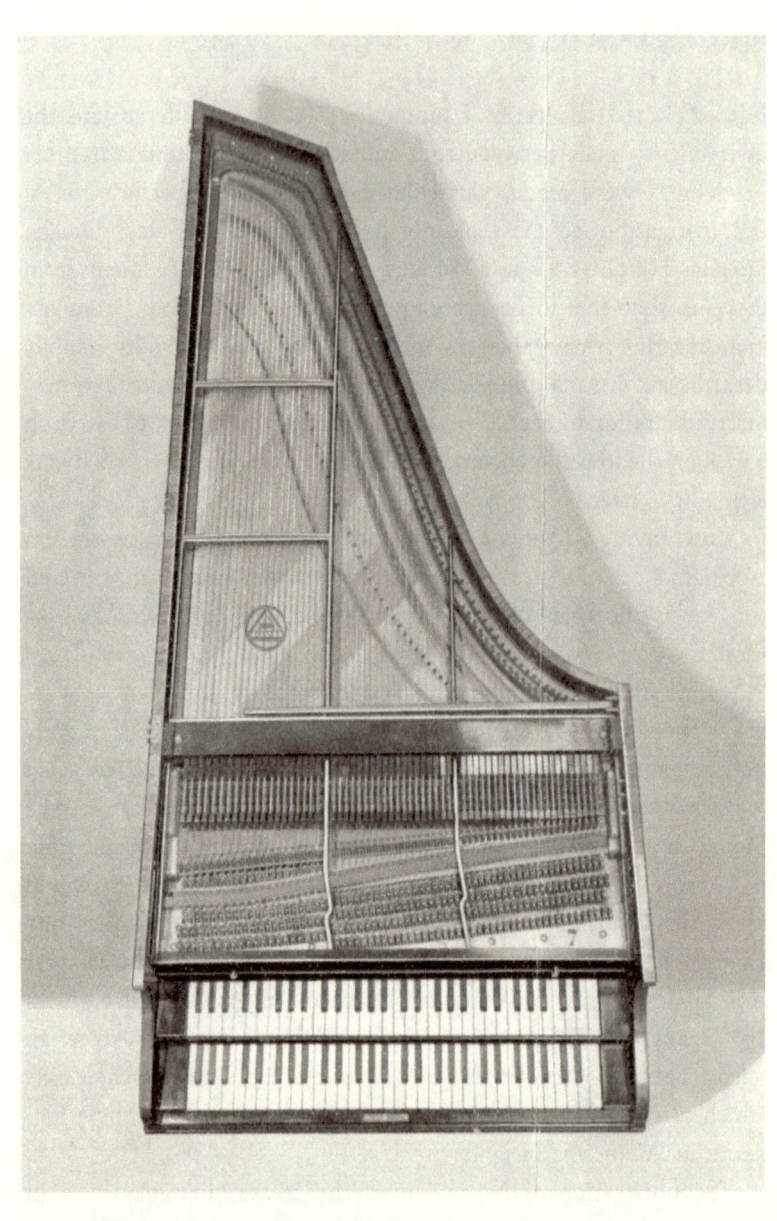

Pleyel Grand Modèle de Concert No 7 – 'Landowska Model'

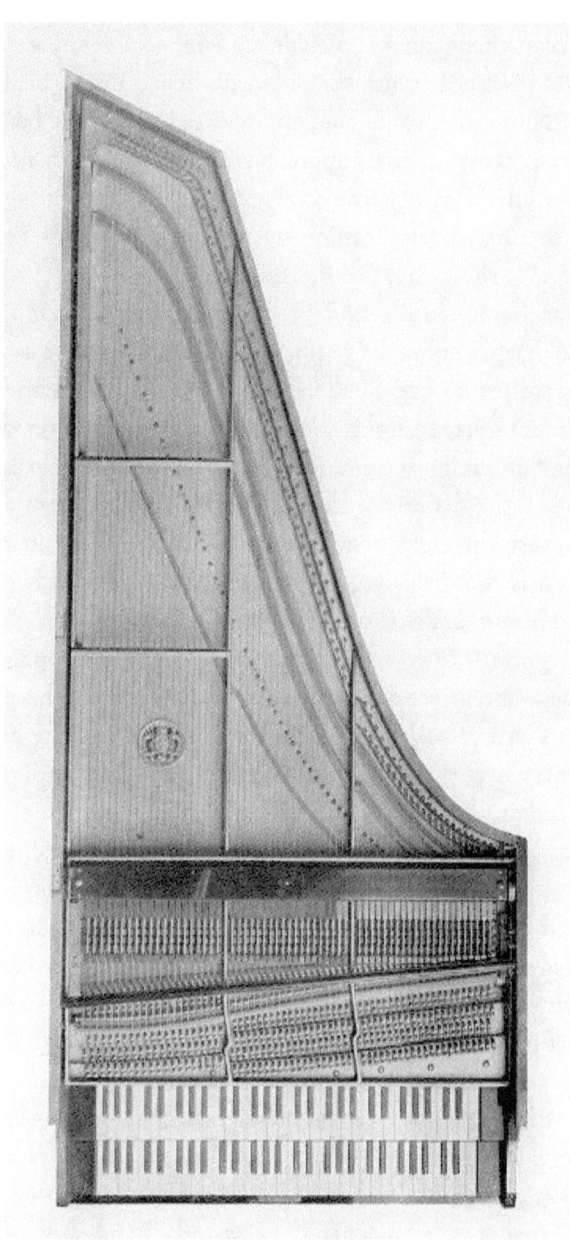

Pleyel Grand Modèle de Concert 1938 – 'Landowska Model'

rose has been changed from a trade transfer to a genuine cast rose, and the harpsichord frame shows no number. The 4′ bridge now travels without curve to its bass end and the photo has been taken directly from above to give a more correct impression of the length of the instrument vis-à-vis the catalogue photo of No. 7, which was taken of the instrument leaning up against a wall and hence the photo shows it somewhat foreshortened.

The iron frame is fully evident. It should be said that although the non 16′ harpsichords did not have a full one piece cast iron frame, Pleyel did resort to considerable metal bracing, the entire wrest plank, for example, being overlaid with a brass plate in order to mount the fine tuning system. However, the early model cases were still prone to the distortion that modern makers refer to as cheek disease, where the right hand cheek cocks up and the instrument looks as if it is about to step out for a brisk walk! The fully cast, one piece, iron frame totally eliminated this problem.

It is important to remember that the design philosophy behind all the best intentioned twentieth century pioneer harpsichord makers was that of seeking to make improvements to the historical instrument, where they felt it was called for. The passage of time had taken its toll on the casework and playability of the originals, few of which had been adequately restored, in fact, most remained mute. Moreover, the major selling points of structural integrity coupled with musical improvements were what the new makers determined was needed to ensure ongoing sales. Still, if one desired 'absolute authenticity,' (surely an expression not in vogue in those early days), an original Kirckman, say, in close to working condition, could still be purchased in a London sale room for around 40 guineas. Be that as it may, the visual effect of the Pleyel's scrolling of the key cheeks, clearly borrowed from the piano, was in tune with the taste of the time, and of course, it cannot be denied that this feature would also allow a better view of the hands of Wanda Landowska, the star performer.

Notable about these Landowska Models were their pedal mechanisms, most of which worked in reverse to what we might anticipate and, indeed, the reverse to what other makers were to later incorporate as standard in their instruments. An explanation may be seen in the simple fact that if the voicing is set up when the pedal is at rest, depressing the pedal moves the plectra away from the strings making the bite of the plectra ever more gentle and avoiding the destructive alternative of the plectra being asked to do more work than could be reasonably expected of them and thereby ruining the leather's elastic memory in just one 'over' pluck. It was Landowska who said: "the art of the harpsichord is in the voicing." Who would contradict this assertion? Her recordings demonstrate a complete understanding of the capabilities provided her by the instrument at her disposal. The overwhelming climaxes she achieved, through touch, timing and immaculate pedal work, were only made possible by first ensuring a precise regulation and voicing of the registers and pedal mechanisms, designed and manufactured to be fool proof in use. So, apart from the Coupler, Lute and Harp Stop, each of the other pedals, when moved up to the uppermost position (that is to say, at rest), ensured its register was fully on and making the loudest sound possible, as pre-set by the voicer and regulator. This explanation is not given with the intention of denigrating Landowska's art, for, as the noted US music critic Virgil Thomson reviewed:

> She played everything better than any one else does.
> One might almost say, were not such a comparison
> foolish, that she plays the harpsichord better than
> anybody else ever plays anything.

A comment should be made regarding the fine-tuning mechanism, which has been thought by piano tuner technicians, and historically oriented modern harpsichord makers, to be totally pointless. As recorded by Pleyel on page 10 of their catalogue, these tuning pins were devised by one J. P. Alibert. Alibert was a French engineer who had registered his design and drawings in 1876, in Berlin, under the title Alibert's Wirbel zum Besaiten der Klaviere. In 1885 this 'ingenious tuning contrivance' won a Bronze Medal in the London International Inventions Exhibition. Clearly Alibert only had pianofortes in mind but the design was adapted by Pleyel for use, exclusively, in their harpsichords. However, it should be recorded that I have seen a crude form of these tuning pins in a late nineteenth century grand piano by the German maker, Jacob Becker, who maintained his factory in St Petersburg.

A translation of the relevant detail from an article in *Dingler's Polytechniches Journal* 1876 (Dingler) reads:

> There have been many attempts, so far without success, to provide the piano tuner with a 'fine tuning system' to eliminate all jerkiness and remove any 'overshooting' of the required pitch. Achieved by avoiding adjusting the original key around which the string is wound, [Alibert refers to this as the 'Voice' key], Alibert has finally managed to construct a device which differs significantly from anything previously invented and which works effectively!

The Alibert fine tuning pins have also been developed, now being supplied with a steel retaining strip to act as a stop for the front of the tuning pin to notch into and allowing a small arc of movement for precise positioning on the wrest plank. The catalogue lists the number of pins as 224, but this is a typographical error as there have always been 244 strings, necessitating 244 tuning pins.

The principle here applied has one enormous and long term advantage which is that there is no metal fatigue imparted to the strings caused by the constant rotating of the tuning pins. The original brass strings on my 1963 Puyana model are all still present

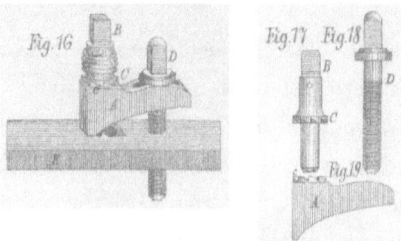

Alibert's Wirbel, engraving 1876

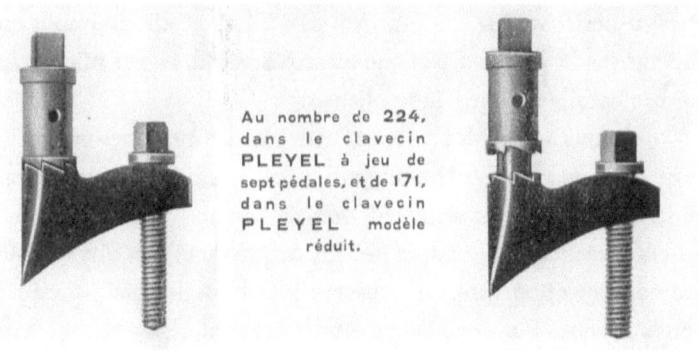

Au nombre de **224**,
dans le clavecin
PLEYEL à jeu de
sept pédales, et de 171,
dans le clavecin
PLEYEL modèle
réduit.

Pleyel tuning pin, 1937 catalogue

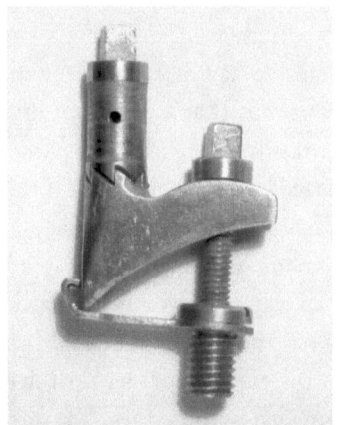

Final development of Pleyel tuning pin, 1963

and are as good as the day they were installed. (In other words they have not broken due to metal fatigue). Which maker, completing his instrument today, would be anticipating such a result?

Another glance at our plan view photograph of No. 7 shows the aesthetic of the keyboards. Critics may say: "the keys are piano styled," however, they are definitely not piano dimensioned. The natural keyheads are 45 mm in length which is within the limits found on original German and Italian instruments. It can be seen that the upper manual sharps are obviously shorter than the lower manual ones, a detail which has practical as well as aesthetic implications. The natural keyheads are of one-piece ivory and, as one might expect, are beautifully finished and polished.

The Landowska Model, then, continued in production for more than forty years. The instruments were not all identical in terms of finish, most were veneered, some of which were inlaid, whilst others were painted, and so on. My acquisition of a Puyana Model provides an opportunity to observe just how flexible a production house such as Pleyel could be, and to record some of the changes both musically and aesthetically. As with other late examples, my instrument is finished in finely figured mahogany but in line with the practice of the 1960s it has a sprayed nitro-cellulose finish which has not weathered especially well. Earlier instruments were French polished. Pencilled on one key of each of the manuals is the word Érard which suggests to me that a degree of division of labour was already present, as a result of the Pleyel-Gaveau-Érard merger. The sharps on my keyboards are not the same profile as on the early Pleyels and might be described as particularly piano like and ugly! However, my instrument does have those ivory naturals, and the whole is finished to an exquisitely high standard.

One change I first thought a matter of taste I now see as eminently practical. The early model had two legs at their tails and the legs were not provided with castors. The later model has one of its tail legs moved to the spine, directly opposite the cheek-bentside junction, which, together with the provision of some extremely elegant castors, provides a far superior 'wheelbase' around the pedal lyre, protecting it, to a degree, from being scraped over uneven floors. Another difference simply reflects our changing lifestyle – there were no rubber buttons attached to the tops of the pedals of the Puyana Model as, after World War II, it became the norm to wear synthetic or rubber soled shoes or, indeed, no shoes at all, hence these buttons could appear redundant. But other non-musical differences might well be described as a matter of taste – for example, my Puyana Model has no lid moulding or inlaid stringing around the case.

More important than the above, however, are the differences which have real musical implications between the models. Perhaps it is required to live and work with the instruments to fully understand the subtleties. One post-war change was that the spine was splayed out towards the tail, widening the tail and necessitating a spacer block between the spine and iron frame halfway along its length, clearly done with the objective of increasing the soundboard area around the bass of the bridges. They may have thought to slim down the appearance of the tail by providing it with only one leg.

The following tables show the pedal dispositions and the differences between the two models.

Landowska Model						
1	2	3	4	5	6	7
16	4	L8	Buff	Cplr	Lute	U8
Buff, Lute and Coupler pedals work in the positive. Depressing the remaining pedals disengages the registers.						

Puyana Model						
1	2	3	4	5	6	7
16	L8	4	Buff	Cplr	Lute	U8
All registers are engaged by depressing the pedals. Additional pedal pressure intended to produce greater volume.						

The end result of the Puyana Model pedal system is that my harpsichord, when I acquired it, needed a complete revoicing, all the leather plectra having been over stressed by every player endeavouring to make the instrument sound as loud as a piano.

The jacks of the lute and upper manual 8′ both pluck the same string and one might reasonably ask why Pleyel did not simply provide one pedal with a pivoting toggle, so that when one register was engaged the other was necessarily disengaged, and vice versa. One reason may be that with separate pedals the player had better control over the dynamic of the pluck within each register, and, in addition, one could actually pluck the one string with two different plectra at the same time. Her recordings demonstrate that Landowska pulled this stunt on a number of occasions, albeit, with somewhat bilious sounding consequences.

Dramatic changes were also made to the soundboard and frame. Instead of the soundboard grain direction being laid at approximately 40 degrees to the spine it now ran parallel to the spine; this obviously also required a subtle adjustment to placement of the ribs attached underneath; even though the soundboard is a three layer spruce laminate. The bass curve to the 4′ bridge has been straightened and the scaling adjusted to give more the appearance and measurement of the historical prototype (Taskin).

The 4′ hitchpin rail is now a separate casting, ingeniously locked in to the major cast frame member, in the manner of composite framed pianos, whereas, formerly, the hitchpin rail comprised simple wooden battens glued both above and below the soundboard. These modifications have the effect of freeing up the soundboard and enabling very light and flexible ribs to traverse the underneath of the board in the manner of current piano making practice and some original Italian harpsichords too, for that matter. The top face of the board no longer sports its trade transfer rose.

Altogether, these modifications make the Puyana Model a very different instrument from the Landowska Model. From an historical perspective, the Puyana Model is perhaps not so interesting, but from a musical point of view, it could be described as somewhat refreshing.

It remains to discuss the overhead dampers. When the key is depressed on a single manual harpsichord every jack rises at the same time and thereby, theoretically at least, lifts all the dampers from their strings at the same time. Therefore, though one or more registers may not be engaged to speak, the unplucked strings of the instrument, are free to resonate in sympathy and so provide useful musical colour. In a double manual harpsichord the full effect of this possibility is lost unless one uses a dogleg jack or an overhead damping system so arranged that any one register of jacks, from either keyboard, removes the dampers from each of the 8' strings whether they are being plucked or not. A careful analysis of the Pleyel shows, without doubt, that this is the main intention of their damping system, and it produces clearly audible results! A refinement not immediately obvious which is offered by overhead dampers in combination with registers operated by pedals, is that at the end of a piece, the 8' registers may be turned off after sounding the last chord, thereby reducing to a minimum the extraneous noise made by the plectra touching their strings on their return to rest. The difference achieved is audible to ear and, more particularly, to microphone.

In conclusion, it may be said that the musical disposition of the Pleyel concert grand harpsichord is based largely on historical precedent and so it is to be hoped that future generations of music historians will treat its creation with a little more deference, even appreciation. Maybe our imagination leads us to believe that musicians of the past regarded their instruments with a good deal more respect and love than can be said of many a modern day performer. Landowska's principal rival in America, Yella Pessl, is quoted by the New York Times, as saying: "I stayed up all last night playing Couperin on my harpsichord; it was almost as good as sex; I said almost!" "Nobody" Rosalyn Tureck said later, "knew more about their instrument, than Landowska."

But let us give Landowska the last word when she described her Pleyel as: "my most intimate confidante."

Note:

Φ Unfortunately, the Pleyel catalogue I have is not dated, however, I happen to know, without doubt, that it dates from 1937. The price list of the two instrument models available was typewritten on a separate sheet of paper and recorded the large concert model to be classified for duty at £560 (Australian Pounds).

Φ It may be seen in the catalogue that Pleyel were prepared to offer their instruments voiced in quill to those who might request it, though it is doubtful (but unconfirmed) if anyone ever actually received an instrument with any of its registers voiced in quill. However, quill was used by Érard in its earliest revival reproductions, which may, in the manner of the times, have prompted Pleyel to present themselves as not in any way lacking in initiative; that their instruments might be considered wholly comparable to that of their esteemed competitor.

PLEYEL GRAND MODÈLE DE CONCERT

The 'Puyana Model' restoration

The complete provenance of my Pleyel Puyana Model, which I acquired in August 1994, is not known. It is believed to have been purchased when new, direct from Pleyel, by the Canberra School of Music, and it was certainly their property for a number of years. Over this time it had been pushed, literally, from pillar to post, and where particularly careless users had managed to put cigarette burns on the right hand key end block and a great many minor scratches and gouges in the casework. Three of the legs had been broken at different times and the School eventually had a wheeled, (rubber tyred), steel, trolley/stand especially constructed, so that the instrument could be easily manoeuvred from one room to another and, of course, on and off stage. The original legs were restored by Mr. Andre Zammit, of the School, and the hideous metal stand has now been discarded for all time.

Around 1979 the instrument was traded in by the School for a French double harpsichord after the work of J. H. Hemsch, by the Japanese piano making firm of Tokai, and the Pleyel became the property of a Canberra piano dealer. Eventually it was acquired privately by Mr. Andre Zammit and then, after numerous entreaties, was purchased by the writer.

The structural integrity of the instrument proper has survived largely unscathed and there is little evidence of wear on the action or keyboard coverings. Ancillary parts such as the music desk and jack rail are in good condition, however, the bottom of the pedal lyre had a section broken off one corner, which has now been repaired. The soundboard and strings were in good condition, except for a large number of 16′ strings where the string sound had gone 'dead' due to the copper windings 'wearing through' and becoming loose on their core. In explanation, the 16′ used covered strings throughout its compass, the windings from FF to c, stop before the string reaches the soundboard bridge, whereas the windings on the remaining strings continued on to the hitch-pin loop. This is not a satisfactory arrangement because the side draft at the points where the strings touch the bridge-pins allows the pins to cut into the extremely fine windings, resulting inevitably in loose windings and dead sound.

A serious and much more time consuming problem concerned the jack tongues. The Canberra School had, at some time, ordered from Pleyel a complete set of replacement tongues (which duly arrived complete with new leather plectra already glued into the tongue holes and presumably ready to voice), however the pivot holes in the tongues were not in the same place as the originals with the result that the plectra were then at different heights under the strings. In order to correct this misalignment the jack bottom screws had been adjusted, but this left the tops of the jacks just as uneven and, as they act as the overhead damper lifters, they are required to be uniformly level and so attempts had been made to rectify this problem by gluing bits of leather or felt to the tops of the jacks. In addition, every plectrum needed replacement due to being over stressed by players stomping ever harder on the pedals. Aside from these items was the fact that the tongues clicked badly on the return of the plectra under the strings which marred the quality of tone of the instrument quite unnecessarily, and which I determined to fix by gluing a leather pad to the bottom of the tongue. Then came the blinding realisation that I was not simply contemplating restoration of the instrument but modifying it to my taste. It was time to make a reasoned assessment of how far I would be prepared to go with my modifications.

The deliberations on how to bring the best out of the Pleyel lasted for some months and, lest I be accused of a gigantic ego trip over the alterations, I decided that each modification had to be justified on the grounds of:

Φ Historical precedent
Φ Correction of obvious errors

Φ The outcome of the application of 1995 building practices according to understood principles of physics, acoustics, mechanics, and/or convention and serious consideration given as to whether their undertaking would yield worthwhile musical gain.

It seemed to me that there should be no room for changes for the sake of current trend or fashion and that if I remained true to the above criteria a more useful and, perhaps, even more interesting instrument would, indeed, be the outcome. If the instrument had been a Landowska Model, there is no doubt that I would have felt somewhat more constrained and to simply restore the instrument as it was when it left the Pleyel factory though, of course, if it were not my property, I would have had little or no say in the matter.

The rationale for my decisions regarding any alterations made during the restoration are detailed below.

BRIDGES AND BRIDGE PINNING

To the historically oriented harpsichord builder, a glance at the Pleyel's 8′ and 16′ bridges shows them to be dimensioned approximately half as big again as any surviving original instrument. Here is obvious piano making technology being applied to the harpsichord, for better or for worse. An advantage might be that the sustain of the sound is so great that one is reminded of French Cathedral organs. Coupled with the extraordinary acoustics of the Cathedrals themselves, French organs produce a swirl of sound that seems to totally envelope the listener. (The Mediaeval/Baroque equivalent of 'surround sound' perhaps?) The sound of my Pleyel sustains for one whole minute. A shortcoming, of course, is that harpsichord music does not call for such an extreme impressionistic possibility and, further, as the Pleyel does not have a sostenuto pedal, like its nephew the piano, the effect can only be appreciated when playing very slowly or when holding down the notes of the last chord of a piece. Moreover, the lighter section bridges evolved by the old masters provided a much sharper attack that carried the pitch of the note to the listeners' ears with great clarity; the effect was accomplished with little regard to the quick attenuation of the tone after the pluck, a logical contention when one considers that to repeat a note on a harpsichord the singing sound of the first tone is necessarily interfered with by plectrum and damper before the string can be made to speak again.

The temptation to pare away the bridges to create a more historical profile I properly resisted, though in the extreme treble, the 16' bridge was so close to the 8' bridge as to be glued to it for the last 4 inches of its length. This, I felt, had to be rectified and the bridges are now separated by a 2 mm gap. The 16' bridge is made of superb quality spruce with a beech capping (this done, no doubt, in order to control the overall mass of the bridge and also to reduce its stiffness, and at the same time the beech capping offering a dense material into which to drive the bridge pins). The greatly differing hardness of these woods made a clean finish of the separation of the bridges, in such a confined space in the treble, so difficult that I realised why Pleyel had left well enough alone. What appeared to be a simple task took well over fours hours. The intention was to free up both bridges enabling them to behave independently so as to provide a better definition of pitch of the notes in that area, and I believe it was worthwhile doing.

Neither the 8' or 16' bridges were double pinned in the treble, though the 4' nut is double pinned throughout. A number of 8' bridge pins were not installed with the same angle as the 16' pins. They were, in fact, leaning slightly forward along the speaking length of the strings, which had the effect of impeding the string's ability to sing; these bridge pins have now been made to conform to the same angles as the majority. It should be noted that the standard of pinning throughout the instrument was very high; there are over twelve hundred bridge, hitch, and tuning pin holes to be drilled and there is only one visible error where a 16' bridge pin was finally positioned on the second attempt! It was decided to remove a bridge pin to better ascertain its material and hardness and they proved to be made from 3/4 hard nickel plated brass, (too hard for my taste, for this hardness factor seems to manifest itself as a slightly hard edge to the sound). Dramatically, the pin that was removed was found to be loose in its hole so a larger diameter, slightly softer pin was substituted with a noticeably more endearing (more musical) result. After a number of other pins were found to be loose it was decided to entirely re-pin all the bridges and nuts. Pleyel's double pinning of the bridges in the bass mirrors that of piano bridge pinning, though, of course, the bridges are not crenellated. The system works perfectly well. I have continued the double bridge pinning to the top note of both 8′ and 16′ bridges, pinned in Pleyel's manner, and this, too, has improved the tone in this area, the after length of these strings, from bridge pin to hitch pin, being excessively long because of the inclusion of the 16′ and needing the control of the extra pinning.

The top surface of the bridges and nuts had originally been coated with a graphite compound, in the manner of piano bridges, and this substance tends to act as a filter between the string and the wood of the bridge destroying the 'presence' of the sound. This was a procedure that old harpsichord makers never utilised, so it was summarily scraped off! Sorry M. Pleyel.

RESTRINGING THE 16′ CHOIR

As noted earlier, the 16′ register used strings that were over wound with copper throughout its compass. From FF to tenor c (20 notes) the windings were contained within the speaking lengths of the strings whilst from c# upwards the windings commenced forward of the nut pins but carried on past the bridge pins to the hitch pins. This is not a good practice as, over time, the windings get flat spots and eventually get cut through by the bridge pins causing false or 'dead' notes. A number of strings in this area exhibited this problem and needed to be replaced. A careful study of the scaling of the 16′

register showed that its scaling was ideal for brass stringing and accordingly, the 16′ now boasts uncovered brass strings from c# to top f‴. String diameters in this section vary from .9 mm for c# down to .4 mm for top f‴, approximating as close as possible the tensions used by Pleyel in their original stringing. To my ear there is no loss of Pleyel quality and all traces of false or dead notes have been eliminated.

RESTRINGING THE 8′ AND 4′ CHOIRS

At this time it was also necessary to consider the bass and tenor of the 8′ stringing, for here, too, over-wound strings were used for the bottom six notes, switching then to plain brass for the four notes BB to D then steel music wire to the top note. Again, unhappily, the over-windings continued past the bridge-pins, and I decided to replace them with appropriate gauge plain brass. At this time I determined, also, to continue the brass up to G. Thus the instrument now has fifteen notes of brass wire, much more in the authentic manner, which in my opinion, yields a simply better sound to the bass than was previously the case.

After much deliberation and experiment a decision was made to change the 8′ strings from steel to iron wire. From a conservationist's point of view all these changes may appear ill-advised, however, what I was aiming to achieve was the best sound possible from the instrument. It surprises me that not all makers believe that an essential nature of harpsichord sound is directly related to the quality of the stringing materials, and there can be no doubt that the steel wire used by Pleyel contributed greatly to the singing nature of their harpsichords and their pianos too, (as noted by Chopin). Nevertheless, this wire was no longer new, and in the larger diameters particularly, surface rust was, to some degree, inhibiting trueness of speech and purity of tone. A conscious decision was made to use Zuckermann plated iron wire which has a slightly higher tensile strength than Rose wire and, being tin-plated, has the laudable property of keeping the rust factor at bay for a considerably longer period of time than unplated iron. This wire was used up to f″, and was kindly supplied by Carey Beebe, then Zuckermann's Australian Agent. The top octave has been restrung in modern music wire, from Marsh Bros., Sheffield, which had also been tin-plated and so matches the Zuckermann in appearance. The outcome of these changes, whilst differing from the original, I consider to be wholly satisfactory and musically worthwhile.

Apart from three notes which were changed because of falseness, the 4′ stringing remains original Pleyel. The ringing timbre of the steel strings seems to me to be more applicable to this register, and offers much greater string life, an important consideration, considering the difficulty in effecting replacements in such models. I am pleased to record that, compared with the original stringing, there has been no discernible change in tuning stability. This is not to say that the instrument does not go out of tune, naturally it does, but simply, that it does appear just as stable as before and that this is unequivocally more stable than the lightly built and strung authentic copy. This is not intended as a provocative assertion but a simple statement of fact occasioned by the string tensions imposed by the instrument's heavier gauge stringing. Wolfenden gives the definitive explanation of the increase in tuning stability accompanying the use of greater string tensions (Wolfenden 1916, 20).

ALTERATIONS TO THE DISPOSITION

The original disposition of the registers of the Pleyel was as follows:

- Φ upper manual 8′ and lute both plucking the longer string to the left.
- Φ 4′ plucking to the right.
- Φ lower manual 8′ plucking the shorter string to the right.
- Φ 16′ plucking to the left.

There are plausible explanations for this arrangement:

Φ Facing the 4′ to the right enabled the scaling to be kept as short as possible, for as far as possible, in the extreme treble of the compass.

Φ By facing the 16′ to the left the scaling could be longer without moving the 16′ bridge closer to the edge of the bentside, which one would have to do to attain the same scaling if the string were plucked to the right.

The arrangement of the 8′ registers was clearly modelled on that of the 1769 Taskin, but it should be remembered that this instrument had the plucking direction of its 8′ jacks reversed at some time in its history, a situation which was not observed by early writers, or makers, and which was not rectified until as late as 1977. Pleyel can hardly be criticised for assuming its 1879 disposition to be original, or rather for not knowing this particular feature of the disposition to be unoriginal. Bearing this in mind I decided to reverse the upper and lower 8′ jacks, without changing the pedal mechanism, with the result that the pedals operating these registers now operate in reverse, i.e. the registers are on when the pedals are up as in a Landowska Model. How serendipitous!

Because the 8′ strings are provided with overhead dampers Pleyel did not provide any of the 8′ jacks with individual dampers, and as a consequence problems of damper interference do not arise. Accordingly, by leaving the lute jacks plucking to the left, it is now possible to use the upper manual 8′ and lute registers in unison, a musical possibility which it is surprising that Pleyel did not exploit. The buff stop was arranged to buff the shorter 8′ string, which means that this register too, is now on when its pedal is up, though it worked in reverse on the Landowska Models. The original buff pads were made of felt and glued to adjustable wooden mounting blocks. Both these have been replaced by a simple buffalo hide pad.

Voicing and regulation

As soon as one looked at the existing state of the original leather plectra one could see big trouble ahead! Many of the tongues had been replaced, but as these had different height pivot holes, the adjusting screws had to be adjusted, almost out of the jacks in the worst cases. Accordingly, I decided to make a complete set of new tongues punched for Delrin plectra for the principal registers and Celcon plectra for the lute stop. Pleyel's preparedness to supply an instrument voiced in quill gave me the licence I needed for this decision, and, too, I recalled Raymond Russell's comment that:

> While quill produces an effect of greater brilliance and clarity than leather when heard at close quarters, the two are very difficult to tell apart when the listener is away from the instrument, as in the concert hall.

The touch, however, is very different. To take full advantage of the naturally incisive possibilities of a Delrin touch, the felt bushings were removed from the pivot points of the keyboards and snug fitting, friction free, wooden 'chasers' were attached in lieu. Both keyboards have their balance point set well to the distal side of centre and Pleyel had leaded the keys heavily so that they returned to their back rest without the weight of the action. Much of this lead has now been removed and the keys individually rebalanced so that the return of the keys to the back rest is only accomplished when the full complement of jacks are in place in their registers and sitting on the keys, in like manner as may be observed in a Kirckman or Schudi.

When reassembling the jacks and their new tongues I decided that the adjusting screws for the tongues were no longer necessary, and these have now been removed; however, small pieces of leather have been glued to both the tongue and the jack body to inhibit, as much as possible, the noise of a tongue's return on release of the key.

When I took delivery of the instrument it was impossible to tell in what order, if any, Pleyel had organised the staggering of the registers. It must be understood that without any staggering whatsoever, the action would feel far too lumpy and heavy, but what can be said is that, by default, the upper manual registers spoke last, simply because of the free play in the keyboard coupling. Too often, it seems to me, instruments provided with a 16' register have that register speaking in the wrong sequence. Hubbard describes the result as an octave drop in pitch and the player: "seeking a nobility and definition of line finds only an inflated and muttering obscurity." When the 16' register is properly voiced and speaking in the correct sequence, however, I don't believe this to be the case. Accordingly, the Pleyel now speaks 4', 16', lower 8', upper 8', lute, and it seems to work! Importantly, too, all the jack springs have been replaced with Nylon covered multi-cored stainless steel, to further remove action noise, (the cause of Kirkpatrick's 'typewriter' criticism).

Finally, all felt listings have been removed and the coupler finely adjusted. The hinges on the spine have been repaired and a new longer lid-stick replaces the original which did not open the lid high enough and lent the instrument an even more piano like appearance. The 'S' shaped keyboard cover is now mounted with loose-pin hinges to the front lid flap, enabling the flap to be folded forward in the manner of original instruments. None of these alterations I have made are of a nature that they cannot be reversed, if someone so desires, and all original parts have been preserved for posterity, including the over-wound strings. Altogether, the task took almost twelve months of work and research and, indeed, was something of a learning experience. I am persuaded that Monsieur Pleyel would have approved, though he might, like a number of others, have asked "Mais porquois?"

CONSIDERING JACKS

Wanda Landowska: "A jack is small piece of wood..."

I refer to the jack as 'my' design, but I am the first to acknowledge that there are no new prophets and that there is nothing original in my design, rather this 'my' is my shorthand in a dissertation on the individual parts making up the whole of the jack.

My jack is made with a closed top, which reduces the possibility of the sides jamming on the tongue. This jamming is one of the most common defects found in jacks, both old and new. The closed top is not difficult to make with a router, set up like a spindle moulder, with the jack blank held in a pivoting arm, which offers the blank to the router blade and thereby ensures precise uniformity of cut for each blank, each and every time. 'Plunge routing' we call it, but the work being offered to the tool rather than the tool to the work. The router bit is up to two inches in diameter with four tungsten teeth, no need for ball bearing.

I have rarely seen a jack removed from a harpsichord other than by grasping it by its narrow sides, which inevitably tends to press those sides together and onto the tongue. Old English jack makers used staples to address this issue, though, of course, the staple also served to limit the backward movement of the tongue. It is surely the individual's choice as to the emphasis he places on either aspect, given his understanding of the parameters. There have been different attempts to seek solutions to these two issues and indeed plastic jacks have gone some way to achieving this, but, it has to be said, with varying degrees of success. It should be noted that jamming of the tongue may occur simply because the wood in the jack body-sides has decided to move of its own volition, which somehow seems even more irritating.

There exist a number of original instruments with closed top jacks, and I have restored one such here in Melbourne, an eighteenth century spinet by Neil Stewart of Edinburgh. In Stewart's jacks the rearward travel of the tongues were limited by staples, whilst the tongues were provided with the usual chiselled angle at their bottom with a similar angle on the bottom of the jack, nicely fitted to provide its purpose of the tongues coming to vertical when at rest. Nevertheless, a large number of tongues required padding to counteract their tendency to slope forward, through pivot wear. Stewart achieved his closed top by gluing an off-cut jack body section into the normally sawn jack wings. The top of the tongue did not touch the glued-in slip at all, its purpose was simply to keep the jack sides the desired distance apart.

A particular advantage of a closed top jack is that it may be designed to offer a secure stop to the forward travel of the tongue. Many times, in original jacks, and modern jacks too, have I seen the tongues leaning forward, past their vertical, which obviously has an effect on the efficiency of their return, and is surely one reason that Ruckers engineered the steep upward angle of up to 15 degrees for the plectra slots in their tongues. The only disadvantage that I can discern from the tongue being stopped at the top is that any noise of the return to stop is more out in the open, as it were, which is to say that the inherent click factor of tongue return is not in any way masked by taking place under the register, in the gap, but rather above it, and therefore just that much closer to one's ear (or microphone). Still, this has not been an issue for me, though I do ensure that the two faces of tongue tip angle and jack top bevel do not touch flat to flat, but at one point only, an effect rather like clapping the palm of one hand with the finger tip of the other.

In my jack, the rearward travel of the tongue is controlled by the spring simply lying down in its groove, which means the tongue doesn't hit anything, (such as a staple, register, or string), so that the backward travel of the tongue's operation is silent and devoid of any click. On the tongue's return to plucking readiness, its face, touching the angled face of the jack top, must be at a different angle, so as to minimise the contact 'click,' an effect which I describe as 'built in applause.' Too sharp an angle on the tongue's top angled face also increases the pitch frequency of any click, with corresponding increase in irritation factor, but this may be minimised by a tiny finishing chamfer, or rounding, on the topmost tip of the tongue's angled chamfer. I have found it important to 'boat' the tongue sides, top and bottom, to avoid any slap of tongue sides against jack wing sides which does tend to occur on tongues with worn pivot holes. The pre-war German maker, Maendler-Schramm, used to punch out tiny little card washers for each side of the tongue to ensure that there was no touching of tongue, jack side to jack side. Maendler, as we know, wanted to provide his harpsichord with a sustaining pedal and, to achieve this with any effectiveness, he had to ensure absolute silence from his mechanism, including the plectrum not touching the string on the jack's return to rest, all of which he achieved. But that is another story...

If there is any point to such meticulous attention to unwanted noise avoidance then it has to be the impression gained that the harpsichord is louder than it actually is, and that there is an increase of clarity provided to the musical line. In other words, there is no music in extraneous noise. Therefore, an attempt should be made to limit the rearward travel of the tongue so that it will strike the jack top on its return to rest with as little impact noise as possible. I have found that there is no need for padding of this stop if the spring is properly adjusted, but there is no doubt that a pad of leather or felt would make the action even more silent, though at the expense of a slightly less precise rest position of the tongue.

My spring is made from multi-cored stainless steel wire, covered with nylon. In this country it is called 'trace' wire, which is used by anglers, between sinker and hook, to stop angry fish from biting through the line, and which I purchase through a local sporting goods store. For me, this wire has several advantages:

Φ Being stainless steel, it will dramatically inhibit rust.
Φ Being multi-cored, it is almost impossible to kink it sharply, rather like trying to kink an electrical

extension lead, so that it is virtually impossible to over tension it as a spring.

Φ The close fitting, nylon sheathing of the core ensures there is silence in its operation, and it looks the part, like a black boar's bristle.

Φ Once the spring tension is set correctly it should never require any further attention in the future, whereas just nylon alone, for example, has too much elastic memory.

So, silence in spring function is important, which the old makers achieved automatically with their Siberian boar's bristles, but bristles are, nevertheless, readily eaten away by hungry and uncaring moths and, over time, tend to lose all of their effective springiness, if not their very existence. The most desirable bristle colour was white, but black was also used, so I think my black nylon looks OK! John Barnes has said that with Kirckman and Schudi jacks, the spring tension was so light that when the jack was held on its back, on the horizontal, the mass of the tongue was not supported by the spring. I do not aim to achieve this level of refinement for I have found that a too weak tongue spring will affect the volume level and the sound of the pluck. Still, bristles were carefully graded for strength by the old makers, thicker, and therefore stronger, for the bass.

The mounting of this wire is simplicity itself: a very slightly larger diameter hole is drilled in the bottom of the tongue, at a right angle to its vertical axis, and about a 1/4″ deep. With a small pair of smooth-jawed pliers, I crimp one section of the wire, just clear of its end, so as to leave an undistorted end portion to centre and slip readily into the tongue hole. The crimped section holds it firmly in the tongue hole, with no glue or wedge. I use the pliers to ease it into the hole, and I use stained glass window makers' lead cutting side cutters (fanlight brand) to cut the spring to length. I have found these cutters, which are sharp enough to cut paper (and damper felt), give a remarkably clean cut with minimum distortion of the nylon covering of the wire. The spring is restricted from falling out because the bottom of the spring-groove in the jack offers it a right angle of resistance. It is important that the hole in the tongue's bottom is not too oversize, because the crimping effect is fairly small and I don't want a loose spring. Over many years of use I have never had a spring fall out, or malfunction in any way, which is surely a bold statement, but true!

The silent operation of the spring itself is mightily important – it is one of the problems affecting the Pleyels, which were provided with old clothes-peg, coil type steel springs, which worked admirably trouble free, but which occasioned Ralph Kirkpatrick to describe the sound of a Pleyel as resembling that of a typewriter. Not being a builder, he was unable to pinpoint the cause and I would agree with him, but I am sure that what he heard is what I describe as spring rattle. I have replaced the original springs with trace wire in my own Pleyel's jacks and have shown this to be the case.

Looking at the design of the tongue itself, I like to consider it being rather bottom heavy on its pivot, that is to say, a large portion of the mass of the tongue is below the pivot point so that when it is moved from the vertical, which happens at the moment of pluck as well as on return to rest position after plucking, this large mass wants it to remain unmoved, but when and if it does move, the pendulum effect helps minimise the movement. Thus the spring tension does not have to be excessive – not too much, not too little. I haven't the language skills to express it any better I'm afraid, but the point is that many makers drill the pivot hole for their tongue far too low in the tongue body – which means that, once moved from its sprung/rest position, the tongue is encouraged to keep moving until the heavier part of the tongue, the top, is below the pivot, where, in terms of its mass, we should expect it to be. So, I taper the tongue above its pivot point to best advantage, leaving the bottom below the pivot as heavy as possible. The back faces of the tongues are tapered and refined before they are separated from their little blanks so that they all appear similar, one to another.

I use a 'slitting saw' for separating the tongues, which is a circular blade designed for cutting the slots in screw heads. Such a blade has virtually no set, and has only 1/32″ blade thickness, so I lose minimal timber in the cutting. I find it very necessary to concentrate on what I'm doing when using such a blade because they can jam the work so readily, and I have continuing respect for my fingers. The tongues are separate units before they have their plectra slots punched and if, as suggested, they are tapered above the pivot for weight reduction, then there is the bonus of less wood remaining that has to be punched through in creating the plectra slot. An appropriate height of the plectra slot from the top end of the tapered tongue is also critical for avoiding breakages incurred by the punching; not enough wood and, pop!

The damper slot in the jack wing should be machined at least 1mm below the height of the plectra slot. This is to enable the bottom edge of the damper to be angled on an upward slope, so that, the register being turned on, it does not snag against the string, which then chooses to act as a spring itself, and tries to return the jack and register to their off position. With wooden jacks too, a slightly deeper damper slot means that there is less likelihood of the damper material being forced to the bottom of the slot, and breaking the slot-wing due to its being over-stressed at that point. Judging by their products, few jack makers or designers seem to have thought this is an important concept for effective ongoing and trouble-free functioning. The straight grained quality of the wood of the jack body is an important factor here also.

Now we come to the pivoting of the tongue, which, for me, is one of the most critical details of all. It seems that there were myriad attempts to address the problem, from beam balance principle to entirely pivot-less designs and ones that 'pop' in and 'spring' in, and so on. In the reproduction of traditional wooden jacks, a number of makers (including Skowroneck) attempt to minimise the work load by avoiding one drilling operation and to my mind this leaves a lot to be desired in the finished product. As far as I've been able to observe, it was not a practice used by the original makers. It doesn't mean that the jacks don't function but rather, they run the risk of an increase in their noise factor, and with attendant lost motion, which, as you will have observed, I think produce musical shortcomings...

Now, we have to determine the pivot material and this, for me, was the 'Neweys Dressmakers Pin' which were curiously described as 'Warranted Rustless Brass,' Neweys established themselves in the UK, lasted for two hundred years, then faltered, and their pins are now no longer available. French Bohin pins are an alternative, .08 mm in diameter, but Chinese pins are often not uniform in diameter. My Newey pins were nickel plated brass, of uniform diameter in manufacture and they had exactly the right taper I wanted, to their pointed end. Steel or iron pins rust and can jam in their pivot hole particularly if the pivot hole has a close tolerance clearance. Brass can develop verdigris after the nickel plating has worn off, but before that eventuality we should be blessed with millions of trouble free plucks! Stainless steel pins are far too hard. Nickel plated brass pins are the preferred solution because they don't rust or develop verdigris and are much easier to file smooth to the jack body after snipping to length.

An engineering friend once pointed out to me that there are three types of fit: a loose fit, a clearance fit, and an interference fit. It is the clearance fit that we are striving for in the tongue pivot hole; too loose and there is rattle and the possibility of tongue sides slapping against jack sides. In addition, where the fit is too loose, the moment the plectrum engages with the string the tongue's first reaction is to travel to the rear of the axle hole which sets up lost motion and this is detrimental to efficiency, both as to feel and volume. I hear myself saying that one can always voice the volume of a good harpsichord down to taste, but it impossible to voice a poor harpsichord up in volume without its weakest quality, or qualities, somehow being heard as dominant, and pivot hole click is one such.

The tongue material is also important. Schudi and Kirckman, for example, used boxwood tongues for 8' jacks in the middle of the keyboard – the jacks which were required to do the most plucking, and therefore required the most re-quilling – because Boxwood is materially tougher and of finer grain structure than Holly, which, however, they were happy to use throughout the rest of the instrument. I don't think this is a necessary consideration if one is using Delrin or Celcon. I have found that there is a fractionally sized pin drill applicable to the axle diameter of choice; the simplest test is to try to rock the tongue sideways on its pivot – if it rocks excessively, and could slap the jack sides, it is too loose! Naturally, one doesn't want the tongues to become super saturated when subjected to high humidity, because then they can sometimes jam up. I just seek perfectly free movement, with virtually no slop.

There are jack makers today who try to simplify the process of assembling jack with tongue, in my view, without success. They drill one hole through both jack and tongue and then another through one jack side and the tongue with its clearance size drill which means that the pin is only held firmly by one jack wing, on one side of the tongue. If the pivot hole is a fraction too big then the whole axle can wobble and is not held firm, and helps contribute to 'built in applause,' and loss of efficiency. In my assembly process:

Φ An interference hole is drilled through both jack and tongue. If the hole is too tight you will discover just how easily the pin is bent.

Φ The tongue is separated from its jack and then has its clearance hole drilled, the existing hole being the guide.

Φ On assembly, the dressmaker's pin is pushed through both jack and tongue until the pointed end of the pin is projecting through the wide side of the jack wing, just enough so as to leave a proportion of the taper inside the jack wing body and therefore retain an admirably tight fit, but still offer a flat spot to be filed flush to the jack body for later pressing out the pivot wire with a tiny flat faced punch, if ever required.

Φ   The pin is snipped either side and filed flat. On close inspection, one should be able to see an obvious difference in pin diameter from one jack side to the other, but with the clearance hole only in the tongue's pivot hole. The jack's interference hole I describe as a firm fit, just large enough to push the pin through without causing any bending of the pin itself, or splitting of the wood. It is a little more tricky to assemble, as there is no movement available to the pivot pin to find the hole in the tongue, but it can be done.

Φ   To remove the axle pin, it should be pushed out with a special purpose made awl, flat ground at its tip, from smaller diameter side out, to larger, that is to say the reverse of its assembly, otherwise there is a risk of enlarging the hole in the jack body. Smooth jawed pliers will assist once the protruding tip of the pivot pin offers purchase.

Now to the jack body itself. It must be of straight and long grained wood which I prefer to have of a dimensional strength that gives some room for mishandling by the clumsy. Also, I have found that one size seems to suit all Northern makes of instrument, bigger perhaps for Italians, but a little lead can always be added. Weighting is by means of a fishing sinker about 1/4″ in diameter. The sinker is placed in the jack with its hole oriented horizontally within the jack hole, so that on being flat-punched tight in the jack, no outward stress is placed on the narrow walls of the jack hole which could cause it to split, while the hole in the sinker will be hidden from critical eyes. The lead should have some shellac dabbed onto it, to retard its oxidisation.

The body of the jack is thick enough to include a reasonable sized adjusting screw, say 5/8" 8BA, 'cheese' head, in brass, should such be thought necessary or desirable. What I like to do is voice the upper manual jacks first and this register will have no adjusting screws, and once that is all correct, then screws on lower manual 8' and 4' jacks, makes their refinement of regulation a little more straightforward. The upper 8' should always remain the unchanging reference. As per Taskin, there is usually a lead weight in my upper manual jacks.

If an adjusting screw is wanted then the jack body is drilled with a drill bit to provide an interference fit for the screw. If the interference hole is the correct diameter then it does not need to be tapped to accept a metal thread screw. Even though I use brass screws which are more liable to twist off, there is never any breakage. To put it the other way, the hole being drilled, then it is a matter of finding the right size screw thread, which is surely a rather more difficult task.

My jacks are not tapered, though of course they can be if that is what is desired, but it seems to me there is little to be gained, and any taper actually reduces the footprint for bottom hole drilling, if one desires to use an adjusting screw. Original tapered jacks were not tapered for considerations of mass, perhaps inertia, but most probably to avoid jamming in the guide slots. It does, however, require some time-consuming register making to attain the same effect as tapering. A piece of straight grained suitable timber, say Linden (Lime), is dimensioned to cover the total number of registers the instrument is to have, let's take three as an example. The wood piece is over double thickness, for it will later be deep sawn, on a band-saw with fine set, into upper and lower guides. Once marked out with the appropriate octave spacing, I drill a 3/8" hole and then 'broach' out the round hole into a rectangular one whilst the timber is still in one piece. This means that the registers and guide holes are absolutely identical and therefore there will be no sticking jacks if the jacks themselves are also identical. But then, they have no say in the matter! The piece is deep sawn and the upper piece then sawn into three registers. Both the registers and guide are relieved hole by hole, with a router bit in a high speed drill press, leaving about a 1/16″ wall thickness for the jack to be in contact with, and, because of the original 3/8″ drilled hole, an enlarged centre for tongue or lead weight clearance. The only problem is that it always seems to me to be a lot of work, but the result is very accurate and I never need to leather the registers out of consideration for fit or noise.

The slightly angled spring slot in the jack is done with a 1/16″ router bit mounted in the drill press, surely easy enough!

In my jacks, it can be seen that the bottom of the tongue leaves an open section to the jack body. This is to enable any modification of the spring tension in case of 'hangers' or whatever. To adjust spring pressure, I use a jeweller's screwdriver with a shallow half-round slot ground into its face, as this helps the spring retain its vertical mode.

In the punching of the plectra slot I aim to achieve an upward slope of five degrees, which is surely not much; not the Ruckers's fifteen degrees, but I am voicing in Delrin or Celcon, not quill.

CATNAP THREE

Gems from old journals

It is hoped that the following extracts (verbatim), from journals in the writer's possession, may prove of more than passing interest.

THE BRITISH MUSICIAN, JANUARY, 1893
A Concert of Ancient Music

From 1776 to 1848 (inclusive) a series of 'Concerts of Ancient Music' were annually given under the auspices of noblemen and gentlemen interested in the preservation of the works of old time composers. A society was established, and the chief rules were that no music composed within the previous twenty years should be played, and that the directors in rotation should select the programme.

At a concert given on the 16th April 1845, His Royal Highness Prince Albert, being the director for that evening, the selection, with one exception, consisted of compositions which had never been heard at the concerts, but the chief attraction was a Concerto composed by Emilie del Cavaliere, A.D.1600, and played upon antique instruments. Their appearance in the orchestra disturbed the gravity of the aristocratic assembly, for, says an eye witness, "truly they presented a strange and grotesque sight". They consisted of a violino Francese, Viol da Gamba, Viol d'Amour, Viol da Braccio, theorbo, violine, guitar, harp and organ, and were played by Messrs Loder, Hatton, Hill, J.F. Loder, Ventura, Dragonetti, Don Cubra, Wright, and Lucas. Most of the instruments, with the music, were forwarded by M. Fetis from Brussels, expressly for the concert, and, says the writer before quoted "the dexterous facility with which the performers adapted themselves to their obsolete constructions was much admired".

The violino Francese was an instrument of the transition period from viols to violins, and had five strings, tuned G.C.F.A.D.

The viol da gamba, as its name implies, was the predecessor of the violoncello, and it has never been completely effaced. It was made in three different sizes, had five or six strings, and the tuning varied. The viol d' amour has been resuscitated during the last ten years, principally through the efforts of the late C. Zöller, bandmaster of the 2nd Life Guards, himself a distinguished performer. It has sympathetic strings of metal, and is better known in its tenor size as viola d'amore.

The viol da braccio was the Tenor Viol: it originally had six strings tuned from G (bottom line bass clef) C.F.A.D.G.

The Theorbo was a large double necked lute, with two sets of tuning pegs, and was chiefly used for accompanying, the Violine was a "big Viola" and was originally designated the "bass viol", but in late years the name was transferred to the Double-Bass. As stated in Groves Dictionary, "in tracing the history of stringed instruments it is necessary to beware of assuming that the same name always designates the same instrument".

The concerto played upon these instruments on the occasion we are recording was a quaint and pleasant production in two movements. This was followed by a Romanesca of the 15th century, deliciously executed by Mr Loder. The next novelty was a Spanish Vilhancics, or Call to Arms (1520) charmingly sung by eighteen young ladies, pupils of the Royal Academy of Music, accompanied by six guitars. Her Majesty the Queen, who was present, was highly delighted with the concert, and honoured Mr Hatton by hearing him play an air on the Viol da Gamba between the parts.

After an existence of 73 years, the "Concerts of Ancient Music" succumbed for want of support. There seems to be a greater interest in musical matters at the present time than was ever known in this country, and judging by the success of the concerts of Mr Dolmetsch it may be assumed that an attempt to revive the "ancient concerts" would meet with support.

In these democratic days, however, recognised musicians (professional or amateur) would have to take the lead, irrespective of their social position. The days of patronage are past.

I am constrained to make some observations:

Φ The presence of Snr. D. Dragonetti [1763–1846], of Double Bass fame, performing with the group.
Φ The somewhat inadequate descriptions of the instruments, with no effort made to record their dates, suggesting an absence of any 'wow' factor.
Φ That no harpsichord was included in the instrumental ensemble though, most probably at that time, there may not have been a serviceable instrument available to the performers,.
Φ The remarkably generous assistance of Belgium musicologist, M. François-Joseph Fétis, in providing

both instruments and music. He, in fact, is known to have owned a Ruckers virginal, though I have no knowledge of whether or not it was maintained in playing condition.

Φ   Grove's Dictionary already being cited as an authority.

Φ   The reviewer's notice, in passing, of the early successes of the thirty five year old Arnold Dolmetsch, who was to go on to make his first clavichord in 1894, and his first harpsichord in 1896.

Φ   The programme of the Concert of Ancient Music dated May 13th, 1789, forms part of the founder's bequest, Viscount Fitzwilliam of Merrion [1745–1816], to the Fitzwilliam Museum Cambridge. Lord Fitzwilliam selected the music for this concert, which was his privilege as a Director. Handel's music was much in evidence. [Formed part of the Museum exhibition, 1974].

THE BRITISH MUSICIAN, FEBRUARY, 1893
A Lecture On Old Claviers by Mr. A. J. Hipkins, F. S. A.

At the eighth annual conference of the Incorporated Society of Musicians, on Tuesday afternoon, 3rd January 1893, at the Venetian Room, Midland Grand Hotel, London, Mr. J. A. Hipkins, F. S. A. gave a most interesting performance on some old claviers. The lecture written by Mr Hipkins, giving an entertaining history of the spinet, harpsichord, and clavichord, was read by Mr. W. H. Cummings, F. S. A.

The following was the list of pieces played by Mr. Hipkins:-

On the Harpsichord:

Pavana, "The Earl of Salisburey"[sic];
Galiardo, W. Byrd;
Galiardo (MS), Thomas Morley;
"Le Bavolet-Flotant", Francois Couperin;
"Le Rappel des Oiseaux", J. P. Rameau;
Air in D minor, with Variations, Handel;
Sonata in G major, Domenico Scarlatti;
Air in G and double keyboard Variations selected
from the 30 Goldberg Variations, J. S. Bach.

On the Clavichord:

Prelude in C major;
"Fantasia Cromatica e Fuga", J. S. Bach.

A fuller account of these instruments will
appear in our next issue.

Alfred J. Hipkins was apprenticed, at age fourteen, to the piano
makers John Broadwood and Sons as a piano tuner, and remained in
the employ of that company all his working life. He was to become a
font of knowledge for those interested in early keyboard instruments
and was widely published. The year 1896 saw publication of his *A
Description and History of the Pianoforte and of the Older Stringed
Instruments* for two shillings and sixpence, much of which is still
relevant today. I find peculiar solace in his logic: from the above
mentioned book, for example, under Harpsichord:

> Excepting the common features of the case,
> soundboard, wire strings, and keyboard, the
> harpsichord differs entirely in sound excitement
> and effect from the clavichord. It has an
> individuality of tone that the pianoforte does not,
> and a certain power, somewhat grandiose, and

brilliancy of effect that the clavichord has not; but in expressive character depending upon the finger, it remains far behind either – indeed, some would deny the harpsichord any expression from the finger. I cannot, however, go with them, as touch must be reckoned with as producing some tone modification, however slight.

THE BRITISH MUSICIAN, MARCH, 1893
An account of the interesting Instruments played upon before the Incorporated Society of Musicians by Mr. A. J. Hipkins, F. S. A.

Virginal or Spinet, Flemish, by Ludovicus Grovelus, lent by Mr. T. Norton. This instrument bears the name of the maker and the date, 1600. The compass of the keyboard is four octaves and a semitone. The soundboard is painted in a conventional fashion, and the rose displays the initials L. G. while the name Pan is beneath the rural God, who is represented blowing an organ in his mouth. The upper keys [the sharps] are beautifully inlaid. The painting inside the cover shows the combat between David and Goliath, and the triumph of David who is received with music. The long flap, which closes the front of the instrument, bears the motto "Sciencia Non Habet Inimiciam Nisi Ignorantem." There has also been a moveable octave spinet in the case, now wanting. The short flap which covered this keyboard bears the motto "Ars Vsv Ivvanda." Spinet, English, early eighteenth century, compass five octaves G – g. Inscribed "Johannis Hitchcock. Londini, fecit, 1676." As in all Hitchcock spinets this is not the date, but the number. The documentary history of this Spinet proves it to have been Handel's. It was presented by Handel to Andrew George Leamon, a violin player, who came to England with him in 1710. The name is probably an Anglicised form of Lehmann. The property of Mr. Hipkins.

Harpsichord, English, inscribed "Burkat Shudi et Johannes Broadwood, Londini, fecerunt, No 1137, AD 1790." Mahogany case, two keyboards, five octaves F – f, three stops to left, two stops to right above keys. Left side of keys another, the 'Machine' stop, upon which the left pedal acts. The right pedal controls the swell shutters, Shudi's "Venetian Swell." Lent by Mr. H. F. J. Broadwood.

Harpsichord, French, Made by Messrs. Pleyel Wolff & Co. of Paris, 1889, and kindly sent from Paris for this lecture, (now on view in New Bond Street). Two keyboards, five octaves F – f, in plain oak case. A rose in the soundboard; six pedals instead of handstops. On the lower keyboard the left or first pedal suppresses the octave, leaving the diapason only. Both these pedals have control of a diminuendo. On the upper keyboard the third pedal from the left governs a muting stop; the fourth is a coupler to the two keyboards, the lower one being played. The fifth is the lute register added to the diapason; it has a crescendo. The sixth has a diminuendo, gradually suppressing the diapason. When the fifth and sixth are quite down the lute only is heard. The use of the pedals is Messrs. Pleyel, Wolff & Co.'s invention.

Clavichord, German Anonymous, of the usual "bundfrei" (fret free) model of the second half of the eighteenth century, lent by Mr. H. Bowman.

Compass five octaves and a fifth, F – c. This was the favourite clavichord of the late Carl Engel.

Clavichord, English. By Peter Hicks, no date. "Gebunden" (fretted). In the upper part of the scale, three notes, and in the middle two notes to each pair of strings, the lowest notes as was customary, single, four octaves and a note C – d. In this fretted instrument the usual free notes in the scale are E and B, instead of the usual D and A. Brass tangents except for the lowest bass notes, which are leather upon iron pins. Black naturals; white sharps – Lent by Mr. T. L. Southgate.

My further observations:

Φ The style of writing has surely much changed during the passage of more than one hundred years, and today, an accumulated core of knowledge of old instruments and their makers, has provided writers with standardized spellings for names of makers, instrument parts, music titles, and much more. An interesting example is that recorded as "Ludovicus Grovelus, spinet of 1600"; as of the present time (2010) we should record: "Lodewijck Grouwels, 'Mother and Child' virginal, 1600." This instrument passed through the hands of Crosby Brown and now forms part of the collection in the Metropolitan Museum of Art, New York. The ottavino 'child,' now residing with its mother, is the work of Arnold Dolmetsch, dating from 1896. Meanwhile, we are left to presume that this virginal was not in a playable condition at the time of the lecture, as none of the works played by Hipkins were recorded, by the journal's correspondent, as having been played by Hipkins on that instrument.

Φ The John Hitchcock spinet was indeed bequeathed by Handel to A. G. Leahmon (most probably originally, Leahmann; Anglicised pronunciation: Lemon) and now forms part of the collection of the Royal College of Music, London.

Φ This is a very late model Schudi & Broadwood harpsichord, number 1137, dated 1790, which was originally supplied voiced with hard leather plectra for the lower 8′ register, the other registers still being voiced in quill. The instrument now forms part of the famous Colt Clavier Collection, in Kent, UK.

Φ How wonderfully accommodating of Messrs. Pleyel to ship to London one of their very earliest harpsichords for Mr. Hipkins's presentation. Clearly Pleyel must have thought the publicity worth the trouble. It is not true, of course, that Pleyel was responsible for the invention of the pedals, however there may be a case if the comment was intended, specifically, to refer to the manner of the pedals' operation, that is to say, mainly in the negative: depressing the pedals turned the plucking registers off, leaving only the lute, buff, and coupler pedals working in the positive. 1889 was Pleyel's first year of harpsichord manufacture; I do not know the whereabouts of this oak cased instrument.

Φ The noted musicologist, Dr. Carl Engel [1818–1882], was the 'Organological Adviser' to the Victoria and Albert Museum for many years, from 1864 until his death. He demonstrated an absorbing interest in early music, as well as instruments, and over time, acquired an unrivalled personal collection, the majority of which he left to the Museum.

Φ This clavichord was bequeathed by Dr Southgate to the Victoria and Albert Museum. There are twenty five pairs of strings to serve fifty-one notes: Boalch records that some doubt exists over the instrument's authenticity.

MORE JOURNALESE

Before the Internet

PIANO TUNER JOURNALS

By rare good fortune I came to possess copies of the *Piano Tuner* for the years 1928–1933, an English monthly trade magazine, just eight years old in 1928 and, as may be imagined, there is much of interest within. It will be remembered that this period saw the Great Depression wrecking devastation on economies around the world. This obviously played heavily on the minds of the compilers of the magazine and, no doubt, those of their clients as well. It is interesting to read that, as early as 1929, mention is made of the anticipated arrival of television, and the implied threat it presented in further clouding the market place for potential purchasers of pianos and allied trades products. A monthly Editorial footnote in the magazines promulgates truisms, many of which seem to me to be as relevant today as when written. Here is but a sprinkling, recorded verbatim, for a little thoughtful diversion:

> The time is probably not far distant when music will stand revealed perchance as the mightiest of the arts, and certainly as the one art peculiarly representative of our modern world, with its intense life, complex civilisation, and feverish self-consciousness. (H.R.Haweis) – [The Rev. Hugh Haweis had published his popular Music and Morals, in 1879. There have been many reprints].

> The laborious attempts by primitive people to construct musical instruments is an indication that music has played an important part in the development of arts and crafts. Had they been

content with the song of the birds, the hum of insects, and forest echos, we should not have made the progress that we have and enjoy its fruits as we do. (Anon).

A fair price is a mutual bargain. (Anon).

It is not at all unlikely that pianofortes will go up in price again. If manufacturers are to remain in business they will be forced to extract bigger profits from a smaller volume of trade. (Editor). August 1931:

Trade is very quiet. We depend on the miners here and they have been doing two days per week. I earned £1 – 18s. – 6d. [$3·85] in June, and August seems to be no better. Things have never been so bad here before. Let us hope we have a busier Christmas Season. (Letter to the editor, from 'C.B.' in Nottingham).

The advertisements in a newspaper are more full of knowledge in respect to what is going on in a State or community than the editorial columns are. (H.W.Beecher).

The golden age, which a blind tradition has hitherto placed in the Past, is before us. (Saint-Simon).

Television is coming; the next entertainment for the home. Television broadcast has been going on regularly for those who possessed the existing expensive sets; but now we shall soon be having a comparatively cheap set making its appearance on the market. (Editor).

It is strange but true, that most of the pleasures of life come from sources uncontrolled by man. (Editor).

Rudolph Dolmetsch gave a recital of harpsichord music at the Grotrian Hall. A delightful afternoon's music, which should have been better attended, brought to London the atmosphere of the sixteenth century. These old instruments, played by one who has made such a study of them, is not only a musical treat but an education, and should be more widely advertised. We are of the opinion that these musical instruments have still a place, for there is music heard at its best on them, and they should not be allowed to become merely an antique any more than the violin is antique, but musical instruments for expressing music of a certain style and period. (Editor, December, 1933).

Arnold Dolmetsch's son, Rudolph, was already presenting himself as being an outstanding young harpsichordist before the outbreak of WW2. He was lost at sea, in December, 1942, aged only thirty six years.

The Monthly Musical Record 1896
Created by British music publisher Augener & Co. in 1871, The Monthly Musical Record existed for almost ninety years. In all the journal comprised 1002 issues, ninety annual volumes and 28,000 pages.

Arnold Dolmetch's first harpsichord of 1896 was praised in the December issue of that year, in an article titled *New and New-Old Musical Instruments*:

> All the unwisdom of all the sages of all the ages seems to have been written about some musical instruments, or accessories to musical instruments, at present or very lately exhibited in London. A note therefore with regard to the respective merits of the viola-ultra, the Schreiber resonator, and Mr. Dolmetsch's new harpsichord, may not be entirely out of place at this moment. The last, belonging to an extinct species, has been hastily dismissed as a mere attempt to reproduce an old model, which assumption we will show to be quite erroneous...

[To record only the comments about the harpsichord]:

> The first two inventions are more or less commercial ventures – intended to fill a want in the market. Not so Mr. Dolmetsch's harpsichord; for although Mr. Dolmetsch makes a harpsichord for those who can pay for it, his instruments are no more "on the market" than, say Whistler's pictures; and Mr. Dolmetsch carries on his harpsichord making rather as an art than as a trade. Probably there will not be a large demand for harpsichord or clavichord for another century to come, if, indeed, the world has learnt by then that the old music should be played on the instruments for which it was written. At the present time no one seems to have grasped the fact that to play Bach's "forty-eight" on the piano gives the listener as erroneous a notion of the effect Bach intended as would be gained of the effect

Wagner intended if the overture to The Flying Dutchman were played on a church organ. Mr. Dolmetsch is doing his best to teach us this great truth, and anyone who doubts it should take the first opportunity of attending one of his chamber music concerts at 6 Keppel Street, Bloomsbury, where he will quickly be converted. Mr. Dolmetsch advocates the use of the harpsichord instead of the piano at performances of Bach's Passions and other choral works; and he has constructed the instrument we are about to describe specially for that purpose. It was recently exhibited at the New Gallery in Regent Street, and was the admiration of all beholders, not merely because of its exquisite shape, but because of the most beautiful paintings with which Miss Helen Coombe has decorated it. The tone is singularly pure and sweet, and quite free from the unpleasant twang one associates with the harpsichord, and it is quite loud enough to fill a large hall. We hope to hear that the Bach Choir will use it at their Bach performances, and we may recommend it to Dr. Martin for the very excellent rendering which he annually gives of the "Matthew Passion" in St Paul's. The new feature of the instrument is Mr. Dolmetsch's contrivance for enabling the player to get crescendo and diminuendo at will. The reader, of course, is aware that the sound is got from the harpsichord by a quill plucking the string; but until now no one has hit upon a method of getting gradations of tone otherwise than with Venetian shutters, as in an organ. But Mr. Dolmetsch has at last devised a piece of mechanism of which neither Ruckers nor any other of the great harpsichord makers need have felt ashamed. We cannot, without the aid of diagrams, describe it in detail. But anyone can understand that if the vibrating string is caught merely by the tip of the quill the sound will not be so loud as when it is caught by the thicker portion near the middle; for in the latter case the string has to be pulled much more to one side before the quill can get free of it. This is the principle of Mr. Dolmetsch's invention. When you wish to play you simply play away, and only the points of the quills touch the wires. But when you press a knee movement you move the quills a little to one side, so that more of the quill catches the wire in passing. The wire is thus plucked more violently, and gives out the desired louder sound. The movement may be held at any place, and thus any degree of sound between pianissimo and fortissimo can easily be obtained. There is no longer, therefore, any excuse for playing Bach and Handel, and, indeed, all the old-world composers, upon instruments which they never dreamed of, and for which their music is very often not at all suited; and, above all, we can now hear Bach's splendid vocal music with something of the instrumental colour he thought of as he wrote it.

Such inventions will be remembered as notable in a century of inventions; not as mere curiosities but as real steps forward; things that are useful now, and will be useful for a long time to come.

BRITISH MUSICIAN APRIL 1893
The *British Musician's* 'Rambler' reported under *Patronage*:

The soprano emanated from the Artistes' room as if she were a pellet from a pop gun, rushed up stairs on to the platform as though like Gilpin she were going for a wager, and with wondrous effusiveness, smiled on us all. I shall never forget that expressive generosity as long as I live. It was grand! The accompanist proceeded with some fifteen bars symphony, and in she came with a terrific fortissimo that caused me involuntarily to take stock of the rafters above, and thank my stars my life was insured. From that moment the lovely smile departed, and there sat upon her features a solid determination. That soprano was going to teach us something: she did, and was encored!

THE BUILDING OF THE PIANO

The typewriting machine, when played with
expression, is no more annoying than the piano when
played by a sister or near relation – Oscar Wilde

The Building of the Piano is the title of the publication by J. Furey,
who titled himself as 'constructor and factory manager' for John
Spencer & Co., piano makers, which book was published by Musical
Opinion, of Chancery Lane, London, in 1929. John Furey records in
his forward that he spent twenty-six years as the Factory Manager
at Spensers,

> ...during which time I have been responsible for the
> making of no less than 60,000 instruments, and
> [which] must necessarily have provided me with a
> wide experience of the difficulties that have been
> overcome in every branch of the business.

I have transcribed the above passage as being worthy of comment
in that no harpsichord maker, living or dead, has achieved such an
heroic output of instruments; neither would he necessarily want to,
of course, but it serves to highlight the activity of our small niche
in an allied craft, and the hunger of the populace, in earlier times,
for cheap and reliable keyboard instruments, the which had grown
to extraordinary proportions by the first quarter of the twentieth
century. Later in the century we were to see electronic organs
experience their 'fifteen minutes of fame,' and more recently, it is
the turn of synthesizer 'keyboards;' when you may simply flick on
the 'on' switch and your choice is a fair representation of the sound
of any instrument you desire, and, should you choose, with a beat
to match. But to return to Mr. Furey for some further insights,
which are the more noteworthy because they are equally applicable
to harpsichord making.

Under the chapter entitled *Bellying*, Furey says:

> For the construction of a good toned piano, the
> first factor undoubtedly is a well designed scale.
> Left to itself, however, the string – the sound or
> tone producer – would give but a poor and feeble
> tone. Something further is required to augment
> or develop the sound produced by the string; that
> 'something' is called the soundboard.
>
> Soundboards have been made of hard woods
> and of soft woods, of aluminium (for which I
> believe, a patent was taken out by a Mr. Pugh), of
> steel, and even of parchment. Double soundboards,
> placed about one inch apart, with large dowels
> between connecting the bridges of the one with the
> other, have been used. Another system of double
> soundboards glued together, with the grain of one
> crossing the other at right angles, the object being
> to dispense with the bars, has also been tried. But
> all these ideas seem to have died a natural death.
> The soundboards in use at the present day are those
> which the experience of years has proved to be the
> most reliable....
>
> It has universally been accepted that the woods
> most suitable for soundboards are Swiss pine,
> Roumanian [sic] spruce, and other kinds of conifer.
> I think myself that, were a number of pianos made,
> each with a soundboard of a different kind of
> conifer, and all parts exactly similar, it would be
> practically impossible to decide which gave the best
> result. All conifers appear to be equally suited for
> this purpose....
>
> At one time it was an axiom in the pianoforte
> trade that soundboards should be thicker at the

treble end than at the bass end; but since the introduction of machinery for the manufacture of soundboards, they have been made of uniform thickness. Personally, I doubt if there is any material difference in tone either way....

The bars should be curved on the side that is glued to the soundboard – a process known in the factory as "bucking". The downbearing on the bridge should never be of such an amount as to force the soundboard below the straight at the back.

Once one has established precisely what Furey means, this latter statement proves to be of some practical use. He actually calculates the ability of the soundboard ribs (bars) to sustain the known or intended downbearing, and sizes his ribs accordingly. His calculations, of course, are only applicable to a piano soundboard but there is relevance to controlling the flatness of a harpsichord soundboard too, for should that not remain stable, the touch and staggering of the harpsichord's action will also be adversely affected.

The New Grove records that the firm of John Spenser & Co. was established in 1884 by John Spenser Murdoch, and made approximately 80,000 pianos in forty years. It would seem then that Furey's claim of involvement with the manufacture of some 60,000 instruments would appear not to be any idle boast. The business ceased during World War II.

It would also seem, from many cases, that earlier generations of makers spent rather more time than we do, in thinking about, posing questions, and proposing explanations, often engagingly written, and which, correct or not, were no doubt intended to contribute to the advancement of the builders' art.

To highlight this claim, one could do worse than quote but one paragraph from Arthur Loesser's *Men, Women and Pianos*:

The harpsichord was provided with one key for each pitch, while into the further end of each key was inserted a wooden upright known as a jack. Into a gap at the top of the jack was built a small pivoting wooden tongue, hinged so as to swing in only one direction. Onto this tongue was fastened a small plectrum – a pick – of either bird's quill or leather. When a key was pressed down, its jack rose, pushing the plectrum against the string from below; with further pressure the elastic plectrum gave way and passed beyond the string, plucking it and producing a tone. When the key was released, the jack dropped and the plectrum again lightly touched the string in its descent; but this time the one-way tongue came into play, swinging outward away from the string; by the time a springy bristle at the back of the tongue made it swing back into its original position, the plectrum had made the little journey around the string and again found itself underneath it. The plectrum's slight descending touch on the string had almost no force, and no second tone was produced; and anyway, a cloth damper at the top of each jack instantly silenced all residual vibration.

And there you have it! However, as it must always have been observed, there shall be a given time-frame for all thought processes to run their course, and for musings such as these, I have to say that this writer's time has almost expired!

COLLECTED CUTTINGS

Changes in realities

From The *First Book of the Gramophone Record* by Percy A. Scholes. [This is an attractive volume, bound, as it is, in full cloth, and blocked with a splendid line-drawing, depicting a wind up gramophone, complete with its wooden-horned speaker].

This volume is an early attempt – I know of no earlier – by an already noted scholar, to offer to the buying public his suggestions for 'fifty must have recordings' from the many thousands of options already available by 1924. The subheading reads: 'giving advice upon the selection of fifty good records from Byrd to Beethoven, a listener's description of their music, and a glossary of technical terms.'

His choice is interesting and includes keyboard music of the Elizabethans with, of course, some Bach and Handel, as well as the expected Haydn, Mozart, Beethoven, and even Schubert. Most surprising is record suggestion No. 5, his inclusion of a Galliard of Dr. John Bull, paired with the Allemande from the Partita in B Flat Major, by J. S. Bach, played on the harpsichord by England's premier harpsichordist, Mrs. Violet Gordon-Woodhouse. The disc is described as a 'small double-sided H. M. V. record, E. 275, 4s. 6d.' [A princely sum indeed: the smaller disc having a diameter of ten inches, as opposed to the larger one of twelve inches. Of course, all discs were then made from shellac, giving them a substantial mass, and were spun by the clockwork turntables of the time, at 78 RPM]. Scholes observes:

> This Bull Galliard is found in the great manuscript collection of keyboard music preserved in the Fitzwilliam Library at Cambridge, being known under the erroneous description of Queen Elizabeth's Virginal Book, but nowadays always called the Fitzwilliam Virginal Book. This book

has come down the ages as a record of the efforts and achievements of the English musicians of its time; the first mention of it is as one of the volumes in the library of Dr. Pepusch, at the sale of which, in 1762, it fetched 10 guineas, which is about the same one has to pay to-day for a second-hand copy of the Breitkopf and Härtel reprint of 1899, which is unfortunately scarce and difficult to obtain. It ought to be a point of national honour to publish both a facsimile edition and an edition in modern notation, and to keep these in print.

The Galliard of this period may to some at first sound a little confused and uninteresting. Listen to it, however, several times, in a quiet spirit, and it will be found to make its effect. Mrs Gordon-Woodhouse's playing differs in a few notes from that of the Fitzwilliam Book, and she has evidently had access to some other manuscript or has herself transcribed the piece from the Fitzwilliam Book, interpreting the notation a little differently from Messrs. Fuller Maitland and Barclay Squire, the editors of the Breitkopf and Härtel volumes.

What a marvellously subtle reproof over the 'variation of notation,' however, this transgression was obviously not one of sufficient moment to warrant exclusion from Dr. Scholes's top fifty.

Suggestion No. 9 is a second offering by Mrs. Gordon-Woodhouse, on 'a large double-sided H. M. V. record, D. 490, 6s. 6d.' Here she has recorded a Gavotte by H. Purcell, a Prelude by J. S. Bach, L'Arlequin by F. Couperin, and Tambourin by J. P. Rameau. On record No. 10 she recorded the Prelude from the Third English Suite by Bach, and The Harmonious Blacksmith by Handel. [Scholes correctly points out that this latter piece should properly be called Air and Variations from the Fifth Harpsichord Suite].

Suggestion No. 7 presents a Prelude, Sarabande, and three Minuets by H. Purcell, played on the pianoforte by Irene Scharrer, on a large double-sided H. M. V. record, D. 622, 6s. 6d. Here the music is noted as being 'from the harpsichord suites,' but there is no other comment offered by Dr. Scholes as to the wayward, even schizophrenic, nature of playing such idiomatic harpsichord music on the piano. Is it possible he was simply unconcerned?

Still, any suggestion of non-concern would be remarkable, for Dr Scholes was pedantic in the extreme, over matters of detail; for example, he notes that the recordings do not present the repeats as were originally intended, where nowadays we expect them to be performed as a matter of course, and so on.

Further, relating to suggestion No. 24, Pianoforte Solos by [Benno] Moiseivitch, Pastorale and Capriccio by Scarlatti, [Domenico], and Gavotte and Variations by Rameau, Scholes says of the Rameau:

> This is a simple and rather plaintive little air, followed by six 'doubles' or variations. The particular treatment of the air in each of the 'doubles' is easily to be traced, and therefore calls for no explanation. The player, performing an old harpsichord piece upon a modern grand piano, has felt at liberty to introduce a few very trifling changes (certain passages played in another octave from that of the original, &c.). All may, perhaps, be pardoned except his addition of a gaudy little flourish up the keyboard in the last bar, followed by a couple of heavy chords. This is 'out of the picture' – and out of the period.

We read in Scholes's forward to the volume:

> Certain gentle rudenesses towards the record companies, to be found in the following pages, require perhaps a little further softening here. It is encouraging to learn from the principal recording companies that most of the older records of the classics are to be gradually withdrawn and replaced, the cut versions, several times disrespectfully alluded to in this book, giving place to complete versions. The first proofs of this book have, with great kindness, been read by the officials of every record company mentioned. One of these, in a very friendly and 'sporting' spirit, writes as follows:

>> We are amused at your remarks under Records Nos. ⋯ and ⋯ , but do you not realize that at the period these were made, our Company, alone among manufacturers, was developing this form of music because of a firm confidence in it, since completely justified? The issue of this Quartet on the small records (at a lower price than the large) was but part of a plan to interest the widest possible public in string quartet music. If, despite these facts, you still consider the terms of your criticism just, let it stand.

[Scholes responded]: I do still 'consider the terms of the criticism just,' and therefore 'let it stand,' but it is fair that this defence, which has a measure of reason in it, should likewise appear.

148

There are still reasons aplenty for retaining Dr. Scholes on the bookshelf...

Violet Gordon-Woodhouse, [1872–1948], originally trained as a pianist, but, influenced by Arnold Dolmetsch, turned to the harpsichord and clavichord. Frederick Delius wrote his *Dance for Harpsichord* for her and in July 1920 she became the first person in the world to make a gramophone record of harpsichord music, played on the harpsichord.

Irene Scharrer, [1888–1971], made her debut at age sixteen and played regularly before the public until 1958. She was noted for a 'beautifully even touch and great refinement of phrasing' (*The New Grove*).

Percy A. Scholes, [1877–1958], was recorded by Grove V as 'having the most extraordinary range of musical knowledge ever written and assembled between two covers by one man,' in referring to Scholes's Oxford Companion to Music.

Some further cuttings must be shared from *Portraits of Musical Celebrities, A Book of Notable Testimonials*, these extracts taken from a volume published by Steinway & Sons in 1926. (Similar volumes had continuously been produced by Steinway since before the turn of the century). A brief forward entitled, *The Immortals and the Steinway*, states:

> Genius, ever yearning for outward expression, demands the perfect medium in which to offer to mankind its God-given inspirations. The painter must have glowing pigments, the sculptor searches out the finest marbles.
>
> Justly indeed has the title "The Instrument of the Immortals" been bestowed on the Steinway piano.
>
> What finer tribute to Steinway pre-eminence could be given than the testimony of the immortal masters of music contained in these pages?

If nothing else, this book, (from the collection of violin maker, Warren Nolan-Fordham), is a wonderful photographic record of ninety three famous musicians, with the small surprise of the inclusion of harpsichordist Wanda Landowska. Her testimony, given during her first visit to the United States of America in 1923, is exactly what we might expect from such a thoughtful person:

NEW YORK, November 10, 1923.
MESSRS. STEINWAY & SONS,
NEW YORK CITY, N. Y.

Gentlemen: I want to tell you how much I admire the Steinway Piano. The sonority of a Steinway is rich, varied and manifold, sometimes of the quality of the deep register of an organ, sometimes voluptuous and caressing like the warmth of reflected gold.
In its sonority the Steinway runs the gamut of romanticism and passion.
Under the hands of the master it becomes as seductive as the refinement and courtliness of an XVIII century marquis.
It lends true atmosphere to a Mozart sonata or concerto, transparent and radiant like an enchanted mirror reflecting the image of a masterwork.
How marvelously it responds in exactitude and promptness to the fervent call of the artist!
Thus, it forms a noble collaboration between the creators of this piano and the interpretative creator-artist, one a complement to the other in the production of a complete oeuvre.

WANDA LANDOWSKA

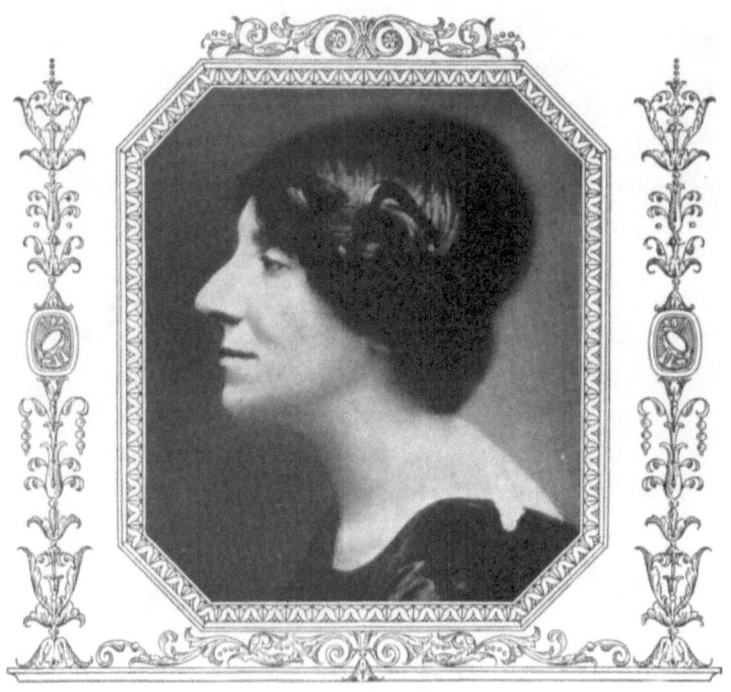

Wanda Landowska

Also included is a letter from Hermann von Helmholtz, the foremost acoustical physicist of the nineteenth century:

MESSRS. STEINWAY & SONS, BERLIN, 1871.

Herewith I beg you to accept my very best thanks for the superb grand piano which you have sent me, and which has safely arrived. I am amazed at the prolonged vibration of its tones, by which the instrument becomes somewhat organ-like, at the lightness and delicacy of the touch (considering its great volume of tone), and at the precise and perfect cessation of the tone which the dampers effect—an element so essential to distinctness in playing. . . . *With such a perfect instrument as yours placed before me, I must modify many of my former expressed views regarding pianos.* I hear frequently many harmonic combination tones; although such a long vibrating tone as that of your grand piano is much more sensitive to dissonances than that of ordinary instruments, the tones of which so quickly die away.

Yours very truly,
H. VON HELMHOLTZ,
Late Professor of Acoustics at the University of Berlin.

Clearly, testimonials were important to Steinway. In closing, the book records:

Some of the Eminent Musical Artists who have used and prefer to use Steinway & Sons' Piano-fortes, and have addressed complimentary letters to our House, which are valued by us as honorary distinctions.

The book's brevity award must go to the famous soprano, Amelita Galli-Curci's one-line classic:

June 22, 1921

When one has known the Steinway – no other can satisfy.

AMELITA GALLI-CURCI.

Over the years, successive, updated editions were published by Steinway & Sons as more and more testimonials were received. Steinway were eager to be associated with the world's finest artists, and ninety three were detailed in this edition. 1926 saw the first appearance of Landowska's contribution though she, of course, continued to play and record on Pleyel pianos as well as those of Steinway. Another 360 names, presumably also adjudged by Steinway to be eminent, were recorded in a separate listing at the end of the volume. Worthy of note in this beautifully printed work is the decorative border that frames Landowska's picture, and the whole clearly evocative of the zeitgeist of the roaring 20s.

ÉDITIONS DE L'OISEAU·LYRE

The Lyrebird in Paris

The following [slightly abridged] article has been lifted from the *Monthly Review of the Record Society (Aust.) Pty. Ltd., Volume 5, Number 1,* of July 1964, as I felt it worthy the retelling:

> Early this year the Australian Broadcasting Commission broadcast a musical feature arranged and presented by Kevin McBeath during which he interviewed Dr. J. Hanson, husband of the late Mrs Louise Hanson-Dyer – founder of the Lyrebird Press, Paris.
>
> We are indebted to the ABC and to Mr McBeath for allowing us to publish this transcript of the interview.

Kevin McBeath: In November, 1962, the world of music lost one of its rarest contributors – rare because the patronage of music has all but vanished with the passing of more gracious eras than our own. What musical patronage is left to us in the twentieth century is primarily given over to the collective and impersonal government of societies, institutions and musical utilities. The musical legacies left to us by the great private patrons of the past – from the clergy, from royalty, from nobility – are part of our accepted tradition of music, to which must now be added the remarkable achievements of an Australian woman musician who devoted a lifetime and fortune to the pursuit of accurate musical research in the twentieth century, and whom we affectionately salute as "the French Lyrebird", a symbol which she has made a familiar part of our broadcasting over the past 30 years.

The lyre is an instrument as old as the harp. Thirteen centuries ago its invention promoted the pleasures we now describe as lyrical. Its unusual contours bequeath an inimitable name to an indigenous Australian bird. Louise Dyer took the bird as a motto to Paris and gave us in exchange a rich heritage of musical patronage such as the last century has rarely seen. What then is the role of the genuine musical patron of our time as opposed to our more automatic and impersonal substitutions? In the present instance, it has been to perpetuate the artistic best that has already emerged from the rich past, to restore the almost forgotten relics of a more distant tradition, and to select from an experimental present the most likely representative milestones for future historians to chronicle. The aural arts have problems associated with no other. Music does not exist outside its own performance and the largest library of scores and gramophone records is incapable of yielding or conveying one note of music until the medium of performance is employed.

And so it was that Louise Bertha Marion Dyer set about to revive both past and principle by establishing in Paris in the early 1930s the Lyrebird Press, an organisation unique in this century's history. With the untimely death of Mrs Dyer we are grateful in the assurance that her work continues under the guidance of her second husband, Dr. Jeffrey Hanson, whose visit to Melbourne last year enabled me to record a conversation with him on the self-appointed tasks and achievements of these two generous Australians.

Dr Hanson, when the history of the Lyrebird Press comes to be written, what would you say would be the most important landmarks?

Dr. Hanson: I think it should be regarded – since you have used the word history – as across time, particularly as a publishing house, of printed music. The recordings have gone around the world. They are extremely important to us and they do make a fine collection, but after all, I'm afraid that recordings – though I would not say they are short lived – have their days numbered in the end.

K. McB: In other words the discs are still regarded as illustrations to your present editions.

Dr. H: I think that is how it should be regarded although the catalogue has wandered a certain distance from the printed music catalogue. I am thinking of the big editions, and the history of L'Oiseau-Lyre should be eventually written around them: editions like the François Couperin, the 13th century, the 14th century, and so on – big library editions which are made available through the universities throughout the world, covering music which would not have been available except for the efforts of the Lyrebird Press. The very first edition put out by the Press was the complete works of Couperin Le Grand in twelve volumes, and this was in 1933, for the bi-centenary of the death of Couperin.

It has certain features which were quite startling at that time. Music publishing at that date – say through the 20s, or from 1900 to 1930, up to the Couperin – music editions then were turned out on the whole in a lamentable manner: poor paper, badly printed, poorly engraved; in other words anything would do for music. That was the situation; and there were distressing features such as the case of an edition of Mozart which did not last fifty years. The paper just fell away to a fine dust and the whole thing went out of existence. So Louise thought of trying something else. She used the finest handmade papers, the best engravers and printers in Paris, one might almost say, in the world, for the engraving of music. The bindings were especially designed by Rose Adler and everything was done to make as permanent an edition as possible. I mean permanent through time – on paper that would last through several hundred years. The bindings are extremely well done, and at the same time the whole thing is very handsome, extremely elegant, and has struck an absolutely new note in music publishing.

K. McB: This edition of Couperin was, I presume, directed towards the collector. Now where does the general music lover come in? Has he access to these editions?

Dr. H: A collector cannot buy anything from the Lyrebird Press. They are not sold in the commercial manner, apart from our usual output of records. I am referring specifically to the limited editions. They are printed especially for libraries, universities, national libraries. Of course, any bona fide scholar who requires them for his work, gets them. That is, even money must not be allowed to stand in his way; but they must not be allowed to get in the hands of collectors and people who put them in their libraries simply because they are so handsome or even obtain them as a sort of speculation. The idea is that they should be in libraries where they can be available to the greatest number. That was the object of publishing the music.

K. McB: Permanency then is the aim for posterity of the Lyrebird Press. The printed editions are directed towards the permanence of the record library and the bona fide scholar, and the recordings – the practical illustrations of the research – remain in the general public's access to the music.

In her preface to her first edition from the Lyrebird Press, Louise Dyer wrote: 'I have determined that an integral edition of Lully's works and of Couperin should be published first, for these two masters are known but in part and their unpublished manuscripts constitute a legacy of French music which it is imperative to save from oblivion. A similar preoccupation has drawn my choice towards the English sonatas of John Blow and Purcell.'

Mrs Dyer arrived in Paris approximately 30 years ago, and apart from her attitude towards the lack of good editions, what else guided her into the misty fields of research?

Dr.H: She went to Paris in 1928, and the first thing she did was to enjoy all the things one finds in the old countries which are not to be found here. In other words, the great works of art, and so on – everything that the old world has to offer. However, she felt that she could not merely sit back and enjoy everything a country has to offer. You must make your contribution; and of course she was a musician of professional standard in her training: she was an excellent pianist, a gold medallist and so on. Music was really her professional career, and she realized that music of the period in which she was particularly interested simply could not be obtained. You could only get the little bits here and there. So she decided she would make it available. And the other aspect was the form which it took – elegance and permanence and so on, which were to her completely natural. That is how she did things in any case. Everything she did was of the greatest elegance – and done with the only thought in mind of its being permanent, and not grandiose, but done on a grand scale just the same.

K. McB: Did you meet any opposition in the early days?

Dr. H: Musicological circles, as you may imagine, are very narrow. There are not so many people in the world who know all about the music of the 13th century; and there are professional jealousies in the formation of teams when there is going to be a big edition of this kind. They formed themselves into two or three camps, but my wife was an expert in dealing with difficulties of this kind. I do not think she met with any special obstacles – perhaps little jealousies – nothing more than that.

K. McB: Mrs Dyer returned many times to her homeland in company with her husband; last year Dr. Hanson returned alone.

Your last visit to Australia two years ago was to promote your new recording of 'Acis and Galatea.' This visit, on the other hand, is occasioned by extremely sad circumstances. I wonder if you would give us some details concerning the terms of the will which were published recently and which include a magnificent gesture towards music here?

Dr. H: My wife devoted her life and her fortune – everything she had – to music and I had the wonderful experience of sharing this with her for the best part of twenty five years. Then came the problem of just how all this was to be handled, were we to disappear, or when we did: and here, it seemed to us, was the solution. The Lyrebird Press of course, goes on under my own direction and the amount of money which my wife has left in Australia, in Melbourne, is to devoted to two purposes. First of all, in my own lifetime, to the continuation of the "Lyrebird Press." On my death the income from this sum, which in round figures is about £250,000 will go to the University for the Louise Hanson-Dyer and J. B. Hanson Foundation for the furtherance of the study of music. The terms are as wide as possible. The University will receive this income and be able to use it exactly as it pleases so long as it is for the study of music. We felt this scheme would complete – come full circle as it were – and continue the work for as long as the present system holds. Incidentally, a gift in the form of a complete set of all the editions and records produced by the Lyrebird Press was made to the Presbyterian Ladies College – my wife's old school.

Outside Australia, I mention Musica Britannica – run by Anthony Lewis, Thurston Dart, etc – musicians and musicologists who also work a great deal with us. My wife very much admired their work and research, and left them a sum of money to express her appreciation and enable them to continue their important work.'

Dr. Jeffery Hanson, as promised, continued to run L'Oiseau-Lyre, single-handedly, until his death in 1971, while the firm continues to the present day. Australia, of course, was to convert to decimal currency on the 14 February 1966, when One Pound became Two Dollars – £1 = $2. More than forty five years ago, $500,000 was a considerable sum of money and the income from same, in perpetuity, did indeed constitute a most generous bequest.

MY LAST HARPSICHORD

An instrument after the important example by Hans Moermans, The Younger, 1642. It is important because of its large compass and 2×8′, 1×4′ registration for such an early date, and also, most particularly, it seems to be one of the earliest instruments made with two aligned keyboards, which means that it had to be conceived as an expressive double rather than the transposing double as normally constructed by Ruckers. It is seen resting on its Ruckers style stand on the stage of its home, the Melbourne Recital Centre, Melbourne, Australia. The final result represents the efforts of Dr. Peter Watchorn, Zuckermann Harpsichords International, and myself.

Such a futuristic instrument appeals as eminently suitable, not only for all early music, particularly Dr. John Bull, but also, for a wealth of later music: one should not forget that early harpsichords existed up to, including, (and after) the time of Bach, Handel, and Scarlatti, but that the later French and English instruments, with their more individual (piano influenced) tonal spectra, did not.

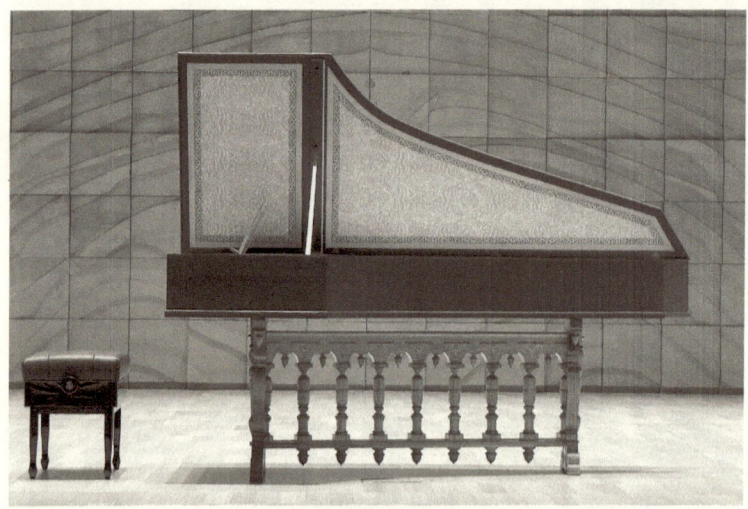

A. R. McAllister after Hans Moermans 1642

162

BIBLIOGRAPHY AND FURTHER READING

Antichi Strumenti. Conservatorio di Musica Luigi Cherubini, Firenze: Palazzo Vecchio, 1981.

Atherton, Michael. *Australian Made... Australian Played...* Sydney: New South Wales University Press, 1990.

Bacharach, A. L., ed. *The Musical Companion*. London: Victor Gollancz Ltd., 1934.

Baines, Anthony. *The Oxford Companion to Musical Instruments*. London: Oxford University Press, 1992.

Barrett, Wm. Alex. *The Great Musicians*. London: Sampson Low, Marston, Searle, & Rivington, 1882.

Blom, Eric, ed. *Grove's Dictionary of Music and Musicians*. London: Macmillan Publishers Ltd, 1961. [Grove V]

Blom, Eric. *Some Great Composers*. London: Oxford University Press, 1944.

Boalch, Donald H. *Makers of the Harpsichord and Clavichord, 1440-1840*. Second Edition by Boalch. Oxford: Clarendon Press, 1974.

Bootle, Keith R. *Wood in Australia. Types, Properties and Uses*. New South Wales: McGraw-Hill, 1983, (12th reprint).

Bridge, J. Frederick (Sir). *Twelve Good Musicians, from John Bull to Henry Purcell*. New York: Kegan Paul, Trench, Trubner & Co. Ltd., 1920.

Briggs, G.A. *Pianos, Pianists and Sonics*. Bradford: Wharfedale Wireless Works, 1951.

Brook, Donald, *Masters of the Keyboard. Illustrated Biographies of 22 Famous Performers*. London: Rockliff, 1947.

Burney, Charles, *The present state of music in Germany, the Netherlands, and United provinces. Or, The journal of a tour through those countries, undertaken to collect materials for a general history of music.* By Charles Burney. London: T. Becket and co. [etc.] 1773.

Byron, May. *A Day with Bach.* London: Hodder & Stoughton Ltd., 1914.

Calvocoressi, Michel-Dimitri. *The principles and methods of Musical Criticism.* London: Oxford University Press, 1931.

Chambers's encyclopaedia: a dictionary of universal knowledge, London: W. & R. Chambers, 1923 – 1927.

Chappell, Paul. *A Portrait of John Bull c. 1563–1628.* Hereford: Hereford Cathedral, 1970.

Clemencic, René. *Old Musical Instruments.* London: Weidenfeld and Nicholson, 1968.

Clinkscale, Martha Novak. *Makers of the Piano, 17001820.* London: Oxford University Press, 1995.

Closson, Ernest. *History of the Piano. Second Edition revised by Robin Golding.* London: Elek Books Ltd., 1947.

Cole, Edward William, ed. *Music.* Melbourne: Sydney: Adelaide: E. W. Cole Book Arcade, 1918.

Cunningham, Walker. *The Keyboard Music of John Bull.* Ann Arbor: UMI Research Press, 1984.

Dale, William. *Tschudi the Harpsichord Maker.* London: Constable and Company Ltd., 1913.

David, Hans T., and Arthur Mendel. *The Bach Reader.* New York: W. W. Norton & Company Inc., revised edition, 1972.

Dingler, J. M., ed. "Alibert's Wirbel zum Besaiten der Klaviere". Stuttgart: *Dingler's Polytechinisces Journal.* 222 (1876): 425–26. Online: http://dingler.culture.hu-berlin.de/article/pj222/ar222113

Dirksen, Pieter, ed. *The Harpsichord and its Repertoire. Proceedings of the International Harpsichord Symposium, Utrecht 1990*, Utrecht: STIMU, 1992.

Dolge, Alfred. *Pianos and their Makers, Volume 2, Men Who Have Made Piano History*. California: Covina Publishing Company, 1913. Reprint by Vestal Press Ltd, New York, 1980.

Dolmetsch, Carl F. *Music and Craftsmanship*. Reprinted from *Fifteen Craftsmen on their Crafts*, London: The Sylvan Press, 1945.

Dowley, Timothy. Bach, *The Illustrated Lives of the Great Composers*. Sydney: Omnibus Press, 1981.

Dunstan, Ralph. *A Cyclopaedic Dictionary of Music*. London: Second Edition, J. Curwen & Sons Ltd., 1908.

Early Music. 1973 – . Oxford: Oxford University Press. [Magazine of 1974 contains first listing of A. McA. as maker.]

Éditions Minkoff. *Musique et Musicologie. [General Catalogue]*, Geneva, 1986.

Ellery, Dr. Reginald. *The Cow Jumped Over the Moon*. Melbourne: F.W. Cheshire, 1956.

Elste, Martin. *Die Dame mit dem Cembalo, Wanda Landowska und die Alte Musik*. Mainz: Schott Music GmbH & Co. KG, 2010.

Erlich, Cyril. *The Piano, A History*. London: J.M. Dent & Sons Ltd., 1979.

Fétis, François-Joseph. *Biographical Note on Sebastien Érard*. Paris: Revue Musicale, X, 1835.

Flower, Newman. *Handel, His Personality and His Times*. London: Panther Books Ltd., 1972.

Foss, Hubert J., ed. *The heritage of music / essays by R. R. Terry [and others]; collected and edited by Hubert J. Foss*. London: Oxford University Press, 1927.

Geiringer, Karl. *Johann Sebastian Bach, the Culmination of an Era*. London: George Allen and Unwin Ltd., 1967.

Geiringer, Karl. *Musical Instruments, their History from the Stone Age to the Present Day*. London: George Allen and Unwin Ltd., 1944.

Gelatt, Roland. *Music Makers: Some Outstanding Musical Performers of our Day*. Sydney: Invincible Press, 1954.

Gerber, E. L. *Historisch-Biographisches Lexicon der Tonkunstler*, Leipzig: 1790.

Gibbia, S. W. *Wood Finishing and Refinishing*. Third Edition. New York: Van Nostrand Reinhold Company Inc., 1981.

Griffiths, J. R. *Musicians and their Compositions (Handel – Bach – Haydn – Mozart – Beethoven – Mendelssohn)*. London: S. W. Partridge & Co., 1895.

Guttormsen, Sissel. *Catalogue of The Ringve Music Museum*. Trondheim, Norway: 2005.

Haase, Gesine. & Dieter Krickeberg. *Tasteninstrumente des Museums*. Berlin: Staatliches Institut für Musikforschung, 1981.

Hadden, J. Cuthbert, *Master Musicians, a Book for Players, Singers and Listeners by J Cuthbert Hadden*, London and Edinburgh: T. N. Foulis, 1913.

Hamilton, David. *The Listeners Guide to Great Instrumentalists*. New York: Facts on File, Inc., 1982.

Harding, Rosamond E.M. *The Piano-forte, its History Traced to the Great Exhibition of 1851*. Cambridge: Cambridge University Press, 1933.

Harrison, Sydney. *Grand Piano*. London: Faber and Faber, 1976.

Haskell, Harry. *The Early Music Revival, a History*. London: Thames and Hudson, 1988.

Hawkins, John. *A General History of the Science and Practice of Music*. Five Volumes. London, 1776.

Heagney, Roger. "Melbourne: City of Harpsichord and Musical Instrument Makers". *Journal of the Institute of Catholic Education*, 5, Melbourne: Institute of Catholic Education, (1984).

Helmholtz, Herman. *On The Sensations of Tone, Translated by A. J. Ellis*. Third Edition. Longmans, Green, and Co., London, 1895.

Henry, Leigh, *Dr. John Bull, 1562–1628*. Tonbridge: Herbert Joseph Limited, 1937

Herbert, A. P. *Mr Gay's London*. London: Ernest Benn Limited, 1948.

Hipkins, A. J. *A Description and History of the Pianoforte*. London: Novello and Company, 1896.

Hogwood, Christopher. *Music at Court*. London: The Folio Society, 1977.

Hollis, Helen Rice. *The Piano – a Pictorial Account of its Ancestry and Development*. Devon: David & Charles Ltd., 1975.

Hoover, Cynthia A. *Harpsichords and Clavichords*. Washington: Smithsonian Institution Press, 1969.

Hubbard, Frank. *Three Centuries of Harpsichord Making*. Cambridge: Harvard University Press, 1965.

Hunt, Edgar, ed. *The Harpsichord Magazine*. Herts: W. G. Kingham, From 1973.

Huskinson, John. *French Music at the Fitzwilliam. (Various Contributors)*. Cambridge: Fitzwilliam Museum, 1975.

Huskinson, John. *Handel and the Fitzwilliam. (Various Contributors)*. Cambridge: Fitzwilliam Museum, 1974.

Isacoff, Stuart. *Temperament*. New York: Vintage Books Inc., 2001.

James, Philip. *Early Keyboard Instruments, From Their Beginnings To The Year 1820*. London: The Tabard Press Limited, 1970. Facsimile of First Edition, 1930.

Jeans, Sir James. *Science and Music*. New York: Dover, 1968.

Kenyon, Max. *Harpsichord Music, a Survey of the Virginals, Spinet, and Harpsichord*. London: Cassell and Company Ltd., 1949.

Kern, Evan J. *Harpsichord Design and Construction*. New York: Van Nostrand Reinhold Company, 1981.

Kottick, Edward L. *A History of the Harpsichord*. Bloomington: Indiana University Press., 2003. [This work also contains a comprehensive bibliography].

Kottick, Edward L. and George Lucktenberg. *Early Keyboard Instruments in European Museums*. Bloomington: Indiana University Press, 1997.

Kottick, Edward L. *The Harpsichord Owner's Guide*. Chapel Hill: The University of North Carolina Press, 1987.

Landowska, Wanda. *Landowska on Music*. New York: Stein and Day, 1965.

Lang, Paul Henry. *Music in Western Civilization*, New York: W. W. Norton, 1941.

Libin, Laurence. *American Musical Instruments in the Metropolitan Museum of Art*. New York: W. W. Norton and Company, 1985.

Lindsay, Joyce and Maurice Lindsay. *The Music Quotation Book, a Literary Fanfare*. London: Robert Hale, 1992.

Loesser, Arthur. *Men Women and Pianos*. London: Victor Gollancz Ltd., 1955.

Loon, Hendrik Willem van. *The Life and Times of Johann Sebastian Bach*. London: George Harrap & Co. Ltd., 1942.

Luithlen, Victor. *Katalog der Sammlung Alter Musikinstrumente. Saiten Klaviere*. Wien: Kunsthistorisches Museum, 1966.

Mellers, Wilfrid, "John Bull and English Keyboard Music", *The Musical Quarterly*, 40, no. 3 (1954), and 40, no. 4 (1954).

Mercier-Ythier, Claude. *Les Clavecins*. Paris: Expodif Éditions, 1996.

Moresby, Isabelle. *Australia Makes Music*. Melbourne: Longmans, Green and Co., 1948.

Mould, Charles. *Makers of the Harpsichord and Clavichord, 1440-1840*. Third Edition. Oxford: Oxford University Press, 1995.

Mould, Charles. *Merlin the Ingenious Mechanician*. London: The Antique Collector Ltd., 1973.

Mould, Charles. *The Development Of The English Harpsichord With Particular Reference To The Work Of Kirkman*. Thesis for the Degree of Doctor of Philosophy. University of Oxford, 1975.

Neupert, J. C. *Historische Tasteninstrumente*. Bamberg, 1985.

Newman, Sidney and Peter Williams. *The Russell Collection of Early Keyboard Instruments*. Edinburgh: Edinburgh University Press, 1968.

Niecks, Frederick. *Dictionary of Musical Terms*. London: Augener Ltd., 1884.

Nurmi, Ruth. *A Plain and Easy Introduction to the Harpsichord*. Alburquerque: University of New Mexico, 1974.

O'Brien, G. Grant. *Ruckers, a Harpsichord and Virginal Building Tradition*. Cambridge: Cambridge University Press, 1990.

O'Brien, Grant. "The Double-Manual Harpsichord by Francis Coston, London, c.1725". *The Galpin Society Journal*, 47, The Galpin Society, (March 1994). [*Coston 1*]

Oughton, Frederick. *Wood Technology*. London: Macdonald & Co. Ltd., 1975.

Palmer, Larry. *Harpsichord in America, a Twentieth Century Revival.* Bloomington: Indiana University Press, 1989.

Parry, C. Hubert H. *Johann Sebaſtian Bach, The Story of the Development of a Great Personality.* New York: London: G. P. Putnam's Sons, 1909.

Paul, John. *Modern Harpsichord Makers, Portraits Of Nineteen British Craftsmen & Their Work.* London: Victor Gollancz Ltd., 1981.

Piano Technicians' Conference. *Secrets of Piano Conſtruction. Reports from the Technicians' Conferences held in Chicago from 16th September, 1916 to 15th, May 1918, inclusive.* New York: The Veſtal Press Ltd., 1985.

Poole, Reginald Lane. *Johann Sebaſtian Bach.* London: Sampson Lowe, Marſton & Co. Ltd., 1884. [Relentlessly, but regrettably, Poole continues propounding the myth that Bach's music had been 'written for the clavichord'].

Prelleur, Peter. *The Modern Musick-Maſter or The Universal Musician, 1731.* Basel: Facsimile by Barenreiter Kassel, 1965.

Prout, Ebenezer. *The Orcheſtra.* London: Augener Ltd.,1897.

Renouf, Nicholas. *A Yankee Lyre, Musical Inſtruments by American Makers.* New Haven: Yale University Collection, 1985.

Renouf, Nicholas. *Musical Inſtruments in the Viennese Tradition: 1750-1850.* New Haven: Yale University, 1981.

Ripin, Edwin M., ed. *Keyboard Inſtruments. Studies in Keyboard Organology.* Edinburgh: Edinburgh University Press, 1971.

Robin, Michel. *Clavecin Goujon – Swanen, 1749 – 1784.* Paris: Société des Amis du Musée Inſtrumental du Conservatoire National du Musée Inſtrumental, 1982.

Rolland, Romain. *Some Musicians of Former Days.* London: Kegan Paul, Trench, Trübner and Co. Ltd., 1915.

Russell, Raymond. *Early Keyboard Instruments: Victoria and Albert Museum*. London: Her Majesty's Stationery Office, 1959.

Russell, Raymond. *Early Keyboard Instruments. The Benton Fletcher Collection, Fenton House, First Edition*. London: The Curwen Press, 1976.

Russell, Raymond. *The Harpsichord and Clavichord, an Introductory Study*. London: Faber and Faber Ltd., 1959.

Sadie, Stanley, ed. *The New Grove Dictionary of Music and Musicians*. London: Macmillan Publishers Ltd, 1995. [*The New Grove*]

Scheurwater, Wouter, and Rob van Acht. *Old Harpsichords, Their Construction and Restoration*. Den Haag: Haags Gemeentemuseum, 1977.

Scholes, Percy A. *The First Book of the Gramophone Record*. London: Oxford University Press, 1924.

Scholes, Percy A. *The Listener's History of Music*. London: Oxford University Press, 6th edition, second impression, 1944.

Schonberg, Harold C. *The Great Pianists, from Mozart to the Present*. New York: Simon and Schuster, 1963.

Schott, Howard, ed. *The Historical Harpsichord, Monograph Series in Honor of Frank Hubbard. Vol. 1 (1984), Vol. 2 (1985), Vol. 3 (1992), Vol. 4 (2002)*. New York: Pendragon Press.

Schott, Howard. *Catalogue of Musical Instruments, Volume 1, Keyboard Instruments*. London: Victoria and Albert Museum. Her Majesty's Stationery Office, 1985.

Schott, Howard. *Playing the Harpsichord*. New York: St. Martin's Press, 1971.

Siepmann, Jeremy. *The Piano. Everyman – EMI Music Companions*. London: David Campbell Publishers Ltd., 1996.

Skowroneck, Martin. *Cembalobau. [Harpsichord Construction.]* Bergkirchen: Edition Bochinsky, 2003.

Stanley, John. *Classical Music*. Sydney: Readers Digest Press, 1995.

Steinert, Morris. *The Morris Steinert Collection of Keyed and Stringed Instruments*. New York: Charles Tretbar, 1893.

Steinway & Sons. *Portraits of Musical Celebrities, A Book of Notable Testimonials*. New York: Publishers Printing Company, 1926.

Stokes, A.W., ed. *The Piano Tuner. The Official Organ of the Pianoforte Tuners Association*. London: White Bros. (Printers). Ltd. 1928 – 1933.

Sumner, William Leslie. *The Pianoforte*. London: Macdonald, 1966, 3rd Edition, 1971. ['The clavichord was a favourite instrument of most of the great composers from 1400 to 1800, including J. S. Bach.']

The British Musician, with which is incorporated The Orchestral Times and British Bandsman. London: F. Howard Doulton & Co., 1893–94.

The Monthly Musical Record. London: Augener & Co., 1871–1960

Thibault, G. (Mme de Chambure), Jenkins, Jean and Josiane Bran-Ricci. *Tour Catalogue of Eighteenth Century Musical Instruments; France and Britain*. London: Victoria and Albert Museum, 1973.

Thomas, Lewis. *The Lives of a Cell: Notes of a Biology Watcher*. New York: The Viking Press, 1974.

Thompson, Oscar. *International Cyclopedia of Music and Musicians, 6th Edition*, New York: Dodd, Mead, 1952.

Turner, W. J. *English Music*. London: William Collins, 1941.

University of Edinburgh. "The Double-Manual Harpsichord by Francis Coston, London, c. 1725". [Data sheet] *Russell Collection of Early Keyboard Instruments*, http://www.music.ed.ac.uk/russell/instruments/hd3fc172520/costonpaper.html [*Coston 2*]

University of Edinburgh. "The Double-Manual Harpsichord by Francis Coston, London, c. 1725". [Essay] *Russell Collection of Early Keyboard Instruments*, http://www.music.ed.ac.uk/russell/instruments/hd3fc172520/datasheet.html [*Coston 3*]

Van Barthold, Kenneth, and David Buckton. *The Story of the Piano*. Edinburgh: British Broadcasting Corporation, T. & A. Constable Ltd., 1975.

Van den Borren, Charles. *The Sources of Keyboard Music in England*. London: Novello and Company Ltd., 1913. [from the original French, published in 1912].

Van Der Meer, John Henry. *Musikinstrumente*. München: Prestel-Verlag, 1983.

Van Leeuwen Boomkamp, Carel, and John Henry Van Der Meer. *The Carel Van Leeuwen Boomkamp Collection of Musical Instruments*. Amsterdam: Frits Knuf, 1971.

Wainwright, David. *Broadwood by Appointment*. Quiller Press, London, 1982.

Wegman, Rob, ed. *The Musical Quarterly Special Issue "Music as Heard"*. Vol 82 no. 3/4. London: Oxford University Press, 1998.

White, William B. *Theory and Practice of Pianoforte Building*. 2nd edition. New York: Edward Lyman Bill, 1909.

Williams, Peter, ed. *The Organ Year Book. Volume 1*. Netherlands: Fritz Knuf, 1970.

Wolfenden, Samuel. *A Treatise on the Art of Pianoforte Construction*. London: Unwin Brothers Ltd., 1916.

Wolfenden, Samuel. *Supplement to A Treatise on the Art of Pianoforte Construction*. Blackfriars: King & Jarrett Ltd., 1927.

Wraight, Denzil. "Neue Untersuchungen an Italienschen Cembali". Köln: *Concerto. Das Magazin für Alte Musik*. February 1986.

Zuckermann, W. J. *The Modern Harpsichord – 20th Century Instruments and Their Makers*. New York: October House, 1969.

www.ingramcontent.com/pod-product-compliance
Lightning Source LLC
Chambersburg PA
CBHW031049180526
45163CB00002BA/746